Consecration in Silence

Consecration in Silence

Dr. ant

This book is not produced, sponsored, authorized,

Table of Contents

A Knightly Consecration to Saint Joseph
by
Dr. ant

Although the author and publisher have made every effort to ensure that the information in this book was correct at press time, the author and publisher do not assume and hereby disclaim any liability to any party for any loss, damage, or disruption caused by errors or omissions, whether such errors or omissions result from negligence, accident, or any other cause.

This publication is designed to provide accurate and authoritative information with regard to the subject matter covered. It is sold with the understanding that the publisher is not engaged in rendering professional services. If legal advice or other expert assistance is required, the services of a competent professional should be sought.

The fact that an organization or website is referred to in this work as a citation and/or a potential source of further information does not mean that the author or the publisher endorses the information the organization or website may provide or recommendations it may make.

Please remember that Internet websites listed in this work may have changed or disappeared between when this work was written and when it is read.

Consecration in Silence: A Knightly Consecration to Saint Joseph

Contents

The Knights' Mission through the Lens of Saint Joseph

Chapter 12: Testimonies of Consecration

Lessons Learned from Devout Followers

Conclusion
Appendix A: Appendix

Additional Prayers and Devotions

Resources for Further Study

Introduction

In the history of Christianity, few saints have garnered the reverence and admiration accorded to Saint Joseph. As the earthly father of Jesus Christ and the chaste spouse of the Blessed Virgin Mary, his life offers a tapestry of virtues and roles that convey the essence of a devout Christian existence. The need for a deeper relationship with Saint Joseph has never been more pressing, especially for those who wish to commit their lives to a higher cause. This manual aims to serve as a guiding beacon for members of the Knights of Columbus, as it weaves together a profound consecration to Saint Joseph.

The Knights of Columbus, a venerable institution within the Catholic Church, embodies the principles of charity, unity, and fraternity. In aligning oneself with the virtues of Saint Joseph, knights can find an exemplar of these very ideals. The act of consecration to Saint Joseph isn't merely a devotional exercise but a spiritual transformation that molds one's life to reflect the holiness, commitment, and fidelity exhibited by the Patron of the Universal Church. Herein lies the importance of understanding the multifaceted character and theologically significant roles played by this humble carpenter of Nazareth.

This manual is structured to guide its readers through various dimensions of Saint Joseph's life and how these aspects resonate with the virtues that every Knight of Columbus should aspire to embody. The introduction serves as a starting point, a place to ground ourselves before delving into the depths of consecration. We set forth on a journey to not merely comprehend Saint Joseph but to integrate his virtues into our daily existence.

Consecration is a theme deeply rooted in Catholic tradition. To be consecrated means to be set apart for a sacred purpose, to dedicate oneself entirely to God's service. Saint Joseph's life was a consecration lived out in silence, action, and fidelity. By aligning ourselves with him, we acknowledge the divine will and accept our own callings with the same obedience and trust that he manifested.

In this ever-changing modern world, the example of Saint Joseph offers timeless wisdom. His role as protector, worker, spouse, and father touches all aspects of human life. He wasn't just a historical figure but stands as an eternal archetype of what it means to live a life dedicated to God and family.

By looking at his example, we can find practical applications to enhance both our spiritual and secular lives.

From the outset, let us recognize that consecration to Saint Joseph involves more than reciting prayers. It entails a commitment to living out the principles he embodied. This means embracing virtues like humility, patience, chastity, and obedience. It involves the daily struggle to align our actions with the moral imperatives that govern Christian life, fostered through devotion, and perpetuated by grace.

Each chapter of this book meticulously unpacks these themes, offering insights into how Saint Joseph's life acts as a blueprint for personal sanctification and communal solidarity. The Knights of Columbus, by their very mission, are called to mirror the virtues of Saint Joseph. Hence, this manual not only focuses on individual growth but also on how to integrate these virtues into the broader objectives of the Knights—charity, unity, and fraternity.

In our exploration, we will delve into the typologies of Saint Joseph, revealing him as protector, worker, spouse, and father. The theological foundations of consecration will be scrutinized to offer a robust understanding that transcends mere ritual and enters the realm of spiritual reality. You'll find pedagogical elements that teach how to live in accordance with the divine will, further anchoring your faith and purpose.

The manual also reflects on the duty of religion, observing commandments, and exemplifying virtues, ranging from humility and obedience to patience and chastity. Principles of natural law, as understood in Catholicism, will provide a moral framework that aligns with Saint Joseph's lived experience. By the end of this journey, included original prayers and devotions will guide you in making your consecration heartfelt and sincere.

One particularly poignant aspect of this manual is its focus on testimonies from devout followers. These personal reflections illustrate how consecration to Saint Joseph has transformed lives, offering real-world examples that inspire and model what is possible through such a profound commitment. In learning from others, you can better chart your own path toward holiness.

The history of the Knights of Columbus is also interwoven with the figure of Saint Joseph. By examining this connection, a clearer picture emerges of how modern knights can carry forward his legacy. This linkage is not just about historical reverence but involves a living, breathing mission that informs every aspect of Knightly endeavors.

As we embark on this sacred journey, let us keep in mind that Saint Joseph serves as more than just a model or a patron; he is a companion in our spiritual quest. May this manual illuminate your path, deepen your understanding, and help you to live a life consecrated to God through the intercession of Saint Joseph. The road to consecration is a pilgrimage of faith, taken step by step, under the quiet yet steadfast guidance of the humble guardian of the Redeemer.

Chapter 1: The Importance of Consecration

The journey of consecration, especially to Saint Joseph, bears profound significance within the Catholic tradition. It's not merely an act of personal piety but a transformative union of our lives with God's divine plan through the intercession of a powerful protector and guide. In recognizing the sanctity and example of Saint Joseph, we align ourselves with a humble servant of the divine will, whose protective care of Jesus and Mary offers a model for navigating our earthly pilgrimage. Consecration redefines our spiritual compass, setting Saint Joseph as a paternal figure whose virtues—humility, obedience, chastity, and patience—resonate deeply with our vocation as Knights of Columbus, aiming to uphold and live out the ethos of our faith in every realm of daily life.

Understanding Consecration in Catholic Tradition

The act of consecration holds a venerable place within the Catholic tradition, deeply embedded in the liturgical, spiritual, and sacramental life of the Church. Consecration is fundamentally an act of setting something or someone apart for a sacred purpose. It is not merely a ritualistic tradition but a profound, transformative commitment. The term itself finds its roots in the Latin word "consecratio," signifying something made holy or dedicated to a divine purpose. Within this rich context, understanding consecration encompasses both a theological and practical dimension.

Historically, consecration in the Catholic Church has been an act applied to churches, altars, chalices, and other sacred objects used in worship. However, by extension, it has also been an act involving individuals. The consecration of religious and lay people mirrors the broader intent of dedicating one's life wholly to God. In this sense, it is a solemn invitation to live fully in accord with divine will, embodying commitment, and faithfulness. Personal consecration heightens one's spiritual journey, molding the individual into a vessel of grace.

Consecration to Saint Joseph exemplifies this tradition, channeling the protection, guidance, and intercession of the earthly guardian of Jesus Christ. The Church offers Saint Joseph as a model of virtue and a spiritual father for all Christians. By consecrating oneself to Saint Joseph, the faithful entrust their lives to his paternal care and exemplary righteousness. This particular form of consecration is an acknowledgment of Saint Joseph's pivotal role within the Holy Family and, by extension, his patronage over the universal Church.

The theological groundwork of consecration finds deep resonance in scripture and tradition. Throughout the Bible, we read about various forms of consecration: from the setting apart of the Levites for priestly duties to the Nazarite vow, where individuals dedicated themselves to God's service with special ascetic commitments. Such consecration practices echo the inherent call for holiness and utter devotion to God's purpose.

Moreover, understanding consecration in Catholic tradition necessitates recognizing its sacramental nature. Sacraments are visible signs of invisible grace, and consecration embodies this duality. It is both an outward pledge and an internal transformation. Through consecration, one is not just committing actions or words but their entire being. This complete dedication echoes the sacrificial love demonstrated by Christ himself and the saints who have followed in His footsteps. In this manner, consecration is an intimate participation in the mystery of God's saving grace and love.

Within the monastic tradition, consecration has a special place. Monks and nuns take vows that are essentially forms of consecration, committing their lives to chastity, poverty, and obedience. These vows transform their daily existences into continuous acts of worship and devotion. Such commitment extends beyond the monastic walls and into the broader experience of Christian life.

Every Christian, in their unique vocation, is called to this consecration—a profound alignment of life and will with God's purposes.

Allegorically, consecration can be seen as a reflection of the soul's marriage to God. Just as marriage in the earthly sense involves a total giving of oneself to another, so does consecration entail a complete self-offering to the Divine. This sacred union calls for faithfulness, love, and unwavering commitment. Within the sacrificial covenant, the consecrated individual finds grace, strength, and purpose, continually nurtured by the Holy Spirit.

Philosophically, consecration touches on the nature of human existence, the search for meaning, and the journey towards ultimate truth. It asks profound questions about one's purpose and the nature of holiness. Through consecration, the individual is not just reaching upwards to the Divine but is also being reshaped by Divine grace into the image of Christ. This transformative process highlights the dynamic interplay of grace and free will, where human effort meets divine initiative.

It's essential to understand that consecration is not a one-time event but an ongoing journey. The daily renewal of one's consecration is vital for sustaining spiritual growth and fidelity. It demands discipline, prayer, and an openness to God's will in every aspect of life. Along this journey, the faithful draw inspiration from the lives of the saints, especially Saint Joseph, who exemplified unwavering trust in God through every challenge.

In the liturgical calendar, the Church provides various opportunities for the faithful to renew and deepen their consecration. Feasts dedicated to the Holy Family, Saint Joseph, and Our Lady invite believers to revisit and recommit to their promises. These liturgical moments are not mere commemorations but are infused with grace, drawing the faithful more deeply into the mystery of divine love and dedication.

Furthermore, in the context of consecration to Saint Joseph, there is a particular emphasis on his titles such as "Guardian of the Redeemer" and "Patron of the Universal Church." These titles encapsulate his unique role and the special graces associated with his intercession. Consecrating oneself to Saint Joseph is, therefore, an act of seeking his paternal protection and guidance, to live virtuously and in faithful service to God.

Modern devotion to Saint Joseph has been enriched by papal endorsements and theological reflections, particularly in recent years. Popes have highlighted Saint Joseph's model of silent strength, obedient faith, and diligent labor. These attributes resonate deeply in a world where faithful Christian witness can sometimes feel like swimming against the tide. Within this contemporary context, consecration to Saint Joseph becomes a source of encouragement and a call to embody these virtues in everyday life.

In conclusion, understanding consecration in the Catholic tradition involves recognizing it as a sacred, transformative, and ongoing act of dedication. It's about setting oneself apart for God's service, inspired and supported by the example and intercession of those who have walked the path of holiness before us. Through consecration, the faithful align themselves more closely with God's will, participating in the divine mystery of love, grace, and redemption. As such, consecration to Saint Joseph is a profound commitment—a step along the path of sanctification, guided by his paternal care and underpinned by a deep theological foundation.

The Role of Saint Joseph in Consecration

The role of Saint Joseph in consecration is a profound and multifaceted one, deeply woven into the fabric of Catholic tradition and spirituality. Saint Joseph, as the earthly father of Jesus and the chaste spouse of the Virgin Mary, embodies a unique combination of virtues that make him an exemplary figure for consecration. To consecrate oneself to Saint Joseph is to commit to a spiritual journey that aligns closely with the divine will, seeking his intercession and guidance in the pursuit of holiness.

Consecration, in its essence, means setting oneself apart for a sacred purpose. It is an act of offering oneself wholly to God, a spiritual dedication that permeates every aspect of one's life. Within this sacred context, Saint Joseph stands as a model of total surrender to God's will. His life, as portrayed in Scripture, is one of constant obedience, humility, and unwavering faith. These qualities are the cornerstones of a consecrated life, making Saint Joseph an ideal patron and guide for such a journey.

At the heart of consecration to Saint Joseph is the concept of trust. Joseph trusted in God's plan even when it defied human understanding. From accepting Mary as his wife, despite the societal implications, to fleeing to Egypt to protect the infant Jesus, Joseph's life was marked by a profound trust in divine providence. This unwavering faith invites those who consecrate themselves to him to cultivate a similar trust in God's plan for their lives. Through this, one learns to navigate life's uncertainties with peace and confidence, knowing that they are under the vigilant care of Saint Joseph.

Moreover, Saint Joseph's role as a protector underscores the importance of consecration. In consecrating oneself to Saint Joseph, one seeks his protection from spiritual dangers and temptations. Joseph's protection goes beyond mere physical safety; it extends to safeguarding one's faith and moral integrity. His intercession is a powerful shield against the snares of the devil and the allure of sin, guiding the faithful towards a path of righteousness and virtue.

Joseph's example also profoundly enriches the concept of work and duty within the life of consecration. As a carpenter, Joseph's labor was a form of worship, an offering to God. In the modern context, this aspect of his life calls those consecrated to him to view their daily work as a sacred duty. It is an invitation to infuse every action, no matter how mundane, with a spirit of devotion and excellence. This perspective transforms ordinary tasks into opportunities for grace, aligning one's everyday life with the divine will.

The familial aspects of Saint Joseph's life further illuminate his role in consecration. As the head of the Holy Family, Joseph's life teaches the values of love, fidelity, and sacrifice within the family unit. Those who consecrate themselves to him are called to reflect these values in their own families. By emulating Joseph's virtues, family life becomes a sanctuary of faith and love, mirroring the sacredness of the Holy Family. It speaks to a broader understanding of family as a domestic church, where each member is nurtured in faith and virtue.

Furthermore, Saint Joseph's silent strength offers a profound lesson in humility and hiddenness. In a world that often glorifies fame and external achievements, Joseph's quiet life of service invites the faithful to find beauty in humility and simplicity. Those who consecrate themselves to him are encouraged to seek greatness in hidden service and to find joy in self-giving love. This shift in perspective is transformative, fostering a spirit of humility that is essential for true sanctity.

In addition, consecration to Saint Joseph aligns the faithful with a rich tradition of devotion and intercession within the Catholic Church. It connects one not only with Joseph himself but also with a community of believers who have sought his intercession over the centuries. This communal aspect of consecration provides a sense of belonging and support, as one joins a spiritual family united in faith and devotion.

Saint Joseph's paternal care also plays a pivotal role in the life of those consecrated to him. As the foster father of Jesus, Joseph's fatherly qualities are a reflection of God's own paternal love. This relationship invites the faithful to experience Joseph's fatherly care in their spiritual journey. It is a relationship that offers comfort, guidance, and a deep sense of being loved and protected. This paternal care is especially significant in times of trial and uncertainty, offering a reassuring presence that strengthens one's faith and resolve.

Lastly, consecration to Saint Joseph is not just a personal devotion but a call to mission. Those consecrated to him are invited to embody his virtues in the wider community, becoming living witnesses to his example. This mission includes acts of charity, promoting justice, and engaging in evangelization. It is a call to be a tangible expression of Joseph's humility, obedience, and love in the world, drawing others to experience the transformative power of consecration.

To consecrate oneself to Saint Joseph is to embark on a journey of deep spiritual transformation. It is an invitation to allow his virtues to permeate every aspect of one's life, leading to a closer union with God. Through Joseph's intercession and example, the faithful are guided on a path of holiness, finding strength, protection, and inspiration in their everyday lives. This consecration is a profound act of love and devotion, opening the heart to the boundless graces that flow through the humble carpenter of Nazareth.

Chapter 2: The Typologies of Saint Joseph

As we delve into the various typologies of Saint Joseph, it becomes clear that his roles extend far beyond the simple narratives often recounted. In examining him as protector, worker, spouse, and father, we uncover layers of spiritual and moral guidance essential to our journey of consecration. Joseph, embodying steadfast guardianship, diligent labor, sacrificial love, and nurturing fatherhood, serves as an archetype for the virtues that Knights of Columbus aspire to embody. The multifaceted life of Saint Joseph offers a profound roadmap for integrating faith into daily existence, guiding us to align our actions with divine will and inspiring a deeper commitment to our religious duties. Each typology not only highlights a distinct aspect of Joseph's life but also challenges us to reflect these virtues within our own lives, creating a legacy of holiness that echoes through generations.

Saint Joseph as Protector

Saint Joseph, in his divinely ordained role as protector, epitomizes the strength and vigilance required to safeguard the Holy Family. His protective nature is not merely a historical attribute but a living testament to his unwavering dedication and care. This archetype of protection harkens back to Joseph's pivotal decisions—such as the flight into Egypt—to ensure the safety and well-being of Jesus and Mary. Through both overt actions and silent guardianship, he embodies the principle that true protection stems from profound faith and unyielding trust in divine providence. For the Knights of Columbus, Joseph's role as a protector serves as a paramount model, calling members to a life of vigilance, strength, and moral fortitude, reinforcing the sanctity of family and the spiritual welfare of the community. By entrusting themselves to Saint Joseph, Knights tap into a reservoir of divine protection that guides them through the perils and challenges of their faith journey.

Scriptural Basis for Saint Joseph as Protector pervades the depths of Holy Scripture, illuminating the figure of Saint Joseph in the light of divine providence and paternal guardianship. From the Gospel narratives, particularly those of Matthew and Luke, the character of Saint Joseph emerges as a guardian entrusted with profound responsibilities. These scriptural foundations elaborate not just his role as the earthly father of Jesus, but also as a spiritual safeguard for the Holy Family, and by extension, for the entire Church.

In the Gospel of Matthew, the author vividly portrays Joseph's role in safeguarding the infant Jesus and His mother Mary. This protective role is first apparent in the account of the angelic dream in which Joseph is instructed to take Mary as his wife, despite her unexplained pregnancy (Matthew 1:20-21). Joseph's immediate obedience to the divine command signifies his willingness to safeguard Mary and the unborn Jesus from potential disgrace and danger. This act of protection isn't just a singular event but a profound spiritual and relational commitment, establishing Joseph as a protector par excellence.

The protective dimension of Saint Joseph's role is further amplified in Matthew's account of the flight into Egypt. Here, another angelic message urges Joseph to flee to Egypt with Mary and Jesus to escape Herod's murderous intent (Matthew 2:13-15). Rather than passive compliance, Joseph's response is decisive and swift. Under the cover of night, he leads the Holy Family into a foreign land, showcasing his relentless commitment to their safety. This journey, fraught with uncertainty and peril, highlights Joseph's unwavering fidelity to his protective duty and reliance on divine guidance.

The Gospel of Luke also contributes to the understanding of Joseph as a protector, albeit in more nuanced ways. In Luke 2:4-5, we see Joseph leading Mary to Bethlehem for the census. Although this might seem like a commonplace act of compliance with civil requirements, it underscores his role as a provider and protector. He ensures that Mary, despite her advanced pregnancy, is transported safely and with dignity. In the manger, where Mary gives birth to Jesus, Joseph's presence signals a protective haven amidst humble and harsh conditions.

In Luke's depiction of the Presentation in the Temple, we further witness Joseph's protective guardianship (Luke 2:22-24). He not only adheres to the religious customs to dedicate Jesus to the Lord but also assures Mary's ritual purification according to the Law of Moses. This act is more than ceremonial compliance; it signifies Joseph's protecting and sanctifying presence within the Holy Family, ensuring their alignment with divine precepts.

Another critical incident is found in the narrative of the Finding in the Temple (Luke 2:41-52). Although Jesus remains behind in the temple, engaged in profound theological discussions, Joseph, along with Mary, anxiously searches for Him. When they find Jesus, their heartfelt concern and Joseph's protective instinct manifest poignantly. This episode underscores Joseph's role in safeguarding not just the physical wellbeing of Jesus but also in nurturing His spiritual and devotional growth.

These scriptural passages illuminate the multi-faceted role of Joseph as a protector. His guardianship transcends mere physical safety, delving into spiritual, moral, and emotional safeguarding. He embodies a paternal archetype entrusted with unparalleled responsibility, profoundly shaped by divine intimacy and obedience. Joseph's protective nature is not characterized by mere defense against harm but by fostering an environment where Jesus and Mary can thrive in their divine missions.

In the broader theological reflection, Joseph's protective nature acquires a typological dimension. As the guardian of the Holy Family, he mirrors God's providential care for humanity. Just as Joseph unhesitatingly protected Jesus and Mary through divine instruction, God's guidance and providence lead the faithful through perils and uncertainty. Joseph thus becomes a symbol of divine protection, mediating between the divine welfare and human frailty.

Furthermore, Joseph's protective role extends to the universal Church. As declared in various papal writings, notably in 'Quamquam Pluries' by Leo XIII and 'Redemptoris Custos' by John Paul II, Saint Joseph is celebrated as the Patron of the Universal Church. His singular guardianship over Jesus extends into his spiritual protection over Christ's Mystical Body. This ecclesial dimension of his protection underscores a profound continuity and solidarity between the Holy Family and the Church.

The typology of Joseph as protector also resonates with the sacramental life of the Church. In the economy of salvation, Joseph's protective role parallels the Church's sacraments which safeguard and nurture the spiritual life of the faithful. Just as Joseph provided for and protected Jesus materially, the Church, through the sacraments, provides spiritual sustenance and protection to its members.

In summation, the scriptural basis for Saint Joseph as Protector is anchored in his divinely ordained role within the Holy Family, extending to the wider ecclesial community. His actions, informed by divine revelation and angelic messages, etch a figure of unwavering fidelity, courage, and providential guardianship. As scholars and devotees reflect on these scriptural foundations, the figure of Saint Joseph emerges not merely as a historical guardian but as an enduring archetype of divine protection and paternal care, inviting a deeper consecration and commitment to his spiritual patronage.

Living Under Saint Joseph's Protection invokes a profound sense of security and peace, much like resting in the shadow of a mighty fortress. Saint Joseph, the earthly guardian of Our Lord Jesus Christ and the chaste spouse of the Virgin Mary, embodies the divine assignment of protection in its fullest expression. Across the centuries, his protective mantle has been a source of comfort and reassurance for countless souls within the Church.

Saint Joseph's protection extends beyond mere physical safety; it encompasses a spiritual guardianship aimed at guiding the faithful toward holiness. Entrusting ourselves to Saint Joseph means to continually seek his intercession, asking him to shield us from spiritual dangers and lead us on the path of righteousness. By living under his protection, we are invited to cultivate a deeper relationship with him, seeking his guidance in our daily struggles and triumphs.

One must understand that living under Saint Joseph's protection is akin to dwelling within a sanctuary of divine grace. Much like the Holy Family's home in Nazareth, our spiritual dwelling under Joseph's care becomes a place where love, faith, and obedience flourish. Emulating the domestic holiness that Saint Joseph fostered with Mary and Jesus, we are encouraged to transform our own homes into places of sanctity and refuge.

In moments of uncertainty or trial, invoking Saint Joseph's protection helps fortify our faith. Saint Thomas Aquinas extolled Joseph as the 'protector of Christ's mysteries,' affirming his unique role in safeguarding the initial mysteries of our faith. By seeking Saint Joseph's intercession, we draw from his wisdom and strength, leaning on him as a sturdy pillar during our spiritual journey.

Saint Joseph's protective role also underscores the importance of vigilance and discernment. In safeguarding the Holy Family, Joseph demonstrated keen awareness and responsiveness to divine messages, showing us the significance of being attuned to God's will. Embracing this vigilant spirit, we learn to discern and reject the subtle snares of evil, thereby maintaining our covenant with God.

The Holy Scriptures provide a firm foundation for understanding Saint Joseph's role as protector. From his silent obedience to God's instructions delivered by angels to his swift action in relocating the Holy Family to escape Herod's wrath, Joseph's life is steeped in protective acts. Each scriptural account of Joseph's protective endeavors invites us to trust in his intercessory power, confident that he can similarly shelter us from harm.

It is worth noting that Saint Joseph's protection is not passive but active and dynamic. He does not merely stand guard but also actively intervenes and guides. This is reflected in countless accounts of faithful Catholics who have experienced his aid in dire circumstances, thus reinforcing the belief in his powerful intercession.

In theological terms, living under Saint Joseph's protection is an act of consecration; it is a deliberate commitment to place ourselves under his guardianship. This aligns our lives with the holy virtues he epitomized—humility, obedience, and chastity. By consecrating ourselves to Saint Joseph, we open our hearts to his paternal care and divine protection, finding solace in his ever-watchful presence.

The Knights of Columbus, in particular, are called to model their lives on Saint Joseph's protective mission. As defenders of faith and family, Knights look to Saint Joseph as their heavenly patron, exemplifying his virtues in their advocacy and service. Through him, they gain strength and resolve to protect the sanctity of family and uphold Christian values in society.

Living under Saint Joseph's protection also fosters a profound sense of spiritual fatherhood. Joseph, as the guardian of Jesus, embraced his role with unwavering dedication. In turn, this teaches us the depth and breadth of true fatherhood, one which transcends biological ties and encompasses spiritual mentorship and care. We are beckoned to adopt such a universal approach to fatherhood, viewing all whom we encounter as entrusted to our spiritual care.

In conclusion, to live under Saint Joseph's protection is to reside within the sacred haven of divine love and grace. It is to journey through life with the assurance of his intercession and care, always steering us toward holiness and safeguarding us from spiritual perils. Whether in the quiet moments of prayer or the trials of daily life, invoking Saint Joseph's protection offers a steadfast assurance that we are never alone, always under the watchful gaze of our spiritual guardian. Hence, let us, with hearts full of faith and love, commit ourselves to his paternal protection, trusting in his unfailing support and guidance.

Saint Joseph as Worker

In the context of "Saint Joseph as Worker," we delve into the profound sanctification of labor as exemplified by Saint Joseph. Often perceived merely as a humble carpenter, Saint Joseph's labor transcended mere craftsmanship to embody a divine synergy between work and worship. His work was not just a means of sustenance but a vocation in which he encountered and served God daily. This magnanimous approach toward labor underscores the dignity of work, elevating it as an act of participation in divine creation. Labor was fused with devotion, illustrating that every nail hammered and every plank polished was an offering to the Almighty. For the Knights of Columbus, emulating Saint Joseph's unwavering dedication and sanctity in daily toil can transform mundane tasks into acts of consecration. By embracing Saint Joseph's virtuous work ethic, modern Christians can find spiritual fulfillment and divine purpose in their everyday endeavors.

Labor and Devotion: The Example of Saint Joseph embodies an essential aspect of understanding Saint Joseph's role within the Catholic tradition, particularly within the realm of work and dedication. Saint Joseph, often depicted with carpentry tools, is more than an emblematic figure; he serves as a living testament to the dignity and sanctity of labor. His life offers a profound blueprint for integrating labor with devotion, illustrating how daily toil can be an act of worship and a means of participating in God's creative work.

Saint Joseph's example begins with his unwavering commitment to his craft. Whether working with wood or engaging in more complex tasks that required ingenuity, Joseph approached each duty with meticulous care and profound respect. This devotion to his work wasn't merely about economic survival; it was a medium through which he expressed his reverence for God. By dedicating his labor to the Divine, Joseph elevated the mundane into the extraordinary, showing that every bit of work, no matter how small, has the potential to glorify God.

In his labor, Joseph harmonized two pivotal aspects of human existence—work and faith. Unlike the contemporary outlook that often segregates secular from sacred, Joseph's life provides a compelling argument for their integration. His daily routines were imbued with prayerful intent, transforming every stroke of the hammer, and every measurement into a spiritual offering. It is within this symbiotic relationship between labor and devotion that Joseph exemplifies the highest form of work ethic. For Knights of Columbus, this offers a profound model to emulate, fostering a devotional life that is robust and interwoven with their daily responsibilities.

Moreover, Joseph's role as the provider for the Holy Family underscores the intrinsic value of work in fulfilling God-given responsibilities. As we examine Joseph's life, it becomes apparent that his labor was not merely about self-sustenance but about creating stability for Mary and Jesus. His diligence provided not only physical nourishment but also spiritual fortitude for his family. This dual provision—a mixture of physical and spiritual nurturing—renders Joseph's labor an epitome of holistic care, a virtue that Catholic men are encouraged to embody within their own homes and communities.

Consider Joseph's carpentry as a metaphor for building virtues. His workbench, filled with tools, becomes an allegory for the human soul crafted by virtues. Patience in honing wood parallels the patience needed in cultivating moral strength. Precision in measurements reflects the exactitude required in moral decisions. The persistence in shaping stubborn wood mirrors the resilience one needs when faced with moral dilemmas and trials. In this light, Joseph's workshop becomes a sanctuary where labor and devotion converge, guiding men toward spiritual craftsmanship.

Joseph's labor didn't isolate him from others; rather, it connected him more deeply with his community. By providing essential services through his skilled labor, he embedded himself within the social fabric, living out the call to love thy neighbor. His approach suggests that work, when done with love and dedication, becomes an act of service to humanity, a way of living out the commandment to love one another. Knights of Columbus, in their community engagements, can draw from this ideal, blending their professional skills with charitable acts.

Also noteworthy is Joseph's silent endurance and modesty in his labor. Scriptures offer little detail about his spoken words, yet his actions resonate profoundly. This silence is not an absence but a powerful presence that speaks to the virtue of humility. In an age where labor often seeks recognition and accolades, Joseph's quiet dedication offers a counter-narrative. It emphasizes that the true worth of labor lies not in public acknowledgment but in the quiet fulfillment of God's will. This perspective encourages Catholics to find deeper meaning in their work, beyond societal validations.

Joseph's deeds serve as a somber reminder that the fruits of one's labor may not always be immediately visible. His carpentry skills ensured the well-being of the Holy Family, yet he didn't witness the full fruition of Jesus' mission. This delayed gratification underscores the importance of faith and trust in God's timing. For those engaged in laborious tasks with seemingly little immediate reward, Joseph's story becomes a beacon of hope, encouraging steadfastness and persistent faith. It reassures Knights of Columbus that their labor, infused with devotion, contributes to a larger divine tapestry.

In restructuring the understanding of labor through the example of Saint Joseph, one embraces a more theocentric view where every component of work finds its ultimate purpose in serving God. Joseph's life encourages a rediscovery of the sacredness inherent in daily tasks, fostering a spirituality that sees God's hand in every laborious effort. This perception can transform work from a mere duty into a profound calling, inspiring Knights of Columbus to reimagine their labor as a continual act of devotion.

Finally, labor and devotion are not merely individual pursuits but have communal implications. Joseph's labor sustained the Holy Family, which, in turn, became the foundation for the Church. Thus, the devotion embedded in labor transcends the individual, contributing to the collective spiritual and physical welfare of the community. Knights of Columbus, by aligning their work with such principles, not only better themselves but also fortify the Church and society at large.

Saint Joseph's example of labor and devotion establishes a timeless standard. As we strive to emulate him, we find that work becomes more than a means to an end; it transforms into a perpetual prayer and an act of worship. By integrating Joseph's principles into their labor, Knights of Columbus can indeed contribute to a holistic and sanctified approach to life, aligning every action with divine purpose.

Applying Saint Joseph's Work Ethic to Modern Life serves as a bridge between ancient wisdom and contemporary necessity, guiding us to merge spirituality with daily labor. Saint Joseph's life as a carpenter and guardian of the Holy Family speaks volumes about meaningful toil, underscoring diligence, integrity, and divine purpose.

In our era, defined by rapid technological advancements and an often overwhelming pace, Joseph's example offers a beacon of stability. His legacy is not solely about the labor itself but about the attitude and sanctity brought to the task. Saint Joseph imbued his work with devotion and love, treating his carpentry as a mission rather than mere employment. This reflects a central ethos: work as a form of prayer, a conduit to glorify God.

Understanding Joseph's work ethic begins with his fidelity to duty. He accepted his role without complaint, despite its trials and uncertainties. This willingness to engage actively with God's plan, even in mundane tasks, is a profound lesson for us. Today's jobs might vary from the manual labor of his time, but the underlying principle remains: every task can be an offering to God, sanctifying even the most routine activities.

Reflecting on Joseph's meticulous craftsmanship, we find a model of excellence. His careful attention to detail and pursuit of quality signify more than skill—they speak to a commitment to serve others and honor God. In modern contexts, this translates into pursuing our vocations with precision, whether in artistry, academia, medicine, or manual labor. It's about striving for excellence not for personal glory but as an act of worship.

However, Joseph's work also teaches balance. He integrated his professional duties with his responsibilities as a husband and father, staying true to his familial and spiritual commitments. For contemporary Catholics, this equilibrium offers solace and guidance. The relentless pursuit of career goals should not eclipse our obligations to family and faith. Balancing these roles requires discernment and prioritization, inspired by Joseph's harmonious life.

Moreover, Joseph's work ethic was profoundly relational; it was always in connection to others. His efforts supported Mary and Jesus, reinforcing the importance of community-oriented labor. In today's world, this principle can manifest in how we contribute to communal wellbeing through our occupations and volunteer work.

Another significant aspect of Saint Joseph's approach is his role as a silent worker. Despite his pivotal part in salvation history, Scripture paints Joseph as a man of few words. His actions spoke louder than any proclamation. This quiet dedication contrasts sharply with modern obsessions with recognition and applause. True value lies not in external validation but in the intrinsic merit of our efforts and their alignment with God's will.

Practically, applying Saint Joseph's work ethic involves cultivating virtues such as humility, patience, and perseverance. These attributes counteract contemporary vices like impatience, arrogance, and entitlement. By embracing these virtues, we transform our work environments into realms of peace and productivity, fostering not just professional but spiritual growth.

Consider adopting a practice of reflective prayer during work hours. Saint Joseph likely contemplated divine mysteries even while engaged in labor. Integrating short prayers or moments of meditation throughout the day can shift our focus from stress to serenity, reminding us of the spiritual dimensions of our toil.

Furthermore, Joseph's example encourages us to recognize the dignity of all labor. There is no 'menial' work in God's kingdom; every role articulates a facet of divine creativity and providence. This awareness can revolutionize how we view and engage in tasks that society may deem insignificant, affirming their worth and our part in a larger divine economy.

Finally, Saint Joseph's work ethic is a call to integrity. Whether in small tasks or grand projects, integrity remains uncompromising. In a world riddled with ethical shortcuts and compromised values, Joseph's steadfastness is a call to uphold principles, even when it's inconvenient or challenging.

In summary, Applying Saint Joseph's Work Ethic to Modern Life is not merely about replicating ancient practices but about embodying their spirit. By integrating Joseph's commitment, excellence, balance, relational focus, humility, and integrity into our modern lives, we sanctify our labor, transforming it into a powerful act of worship and witness to the divine.

Saint Joseph as Spouse

Saint Joseph, in his role as spouse, stands as an unparalleled model of sacrificial love and unwavering fidelity. His union with the Virgin Mary presents a sanctified marriage, forged in mutual respect, divine obedience, and profound spiritual intimacy. The couple shared an extraordinary partnership, deeply rooted in their submission to God's will and sustained by a mutual commitment to the sacred mission entrusted to them. Joseph's acceptance of Mary, despite societal norms and potential disgrace, exemplifies a love that is both protective and self-effacing. In the daily realities of marital life, Joseph's actions provide a blueprint for spouses to emulate; highlighting virtues of patience, understanding, and unwavering support. By fostering a household imbued with faith and divine purpose, their holy matrimony becomes a beacon for Christian couples aiming to mirror this sacred partnership in their own marriages, elevating their domestic church to a reflection of divine love.

The Holy Marriage: Saint Joseph and the Virgin Mary occupies a unique and unparalleled place in the sanctity of Christian marriage. Its profundity is often explored in symbolic, theological, and doctrinal realms, providing both a spiritual and practical paradigm for marital life. Understanding this holy union goes beyond the mere recognition of a historical event; it invites believers into a contemplative examination of divine mysteries and virtues exemplified by Saint Joseph and the Virgin Mary.

Saint Joseph stands as an exemplar of the virtues required for a holy marital union. His life with Mary, the Mother of God, was marked by a relentless fidelity, profound purity, and an obedience to God's will. These elements form the backbone of a marriage intended for the glory of God. The sanctity of their union can serve as a template for married couples striving to live out their vocation with holiness and devotion.

First and foremost, their marriage was divinely orchestrated. The Gospel of Matthew states, "Joseph, son of David, do not be afraid to take Mary home as your wife, because what is conceived in her is from the Holy Spirit" (Matthew 1:20). Here, Joseph's acceptance of Mary, despite her miraculous pregnancy, demonstrates a profound trust in God's plan. This acceptance wasn't a matter of blind faith but of courageous commitment. It is in this courage that Joseph's sanctity is revealed, as he prioritizes divine will over societal norms and personal doubts.

The unity between Joseph and Mary portrays the essence of sacrificial love. Their marriage was not centered around personal gratification but existed for the fulfillment of divine prophecy. Joseph's decision to protect and honor Mary, even when societal law gave him the right to abandon her, speaks volumes of his character. His protection of Mary and Jesus extends beyond physical safety; it is a sign of his spiritual guardianship, an echo of God's protection over His people.

In many ways, Joseph's quiet and steadfast devotion to Mary illustrates the virtue of chastity. Their marriage remained chaste, reflecting a unique calling and purpose. This is not to diminish the value of conjugal relations in marriage but to elevate the specific role they played in God's salvific plan. Chastity, in this context, becomes a deeper expression of love that is completely self-giving and fully attuned to God's purposes. This virtue is essential for married life today, one where love is reflective not only in physical union but in mutual respect, understanding, and spiritual support.

The Marian element adds an irreplaceable dimension to their union. Mary, being full of grace, was the perfect spouse for Joseph. Their relationship was one of mutual sanctification. Mary's Immaculate Conception and sinless life worked in synergy with Joseph's righteous and obedient nature. Such a union was predestined by God to bring forth the Savior of the world. In their daily life, we glimpse a perfect harmony of wills united for a divine cause. For married couples today, this calls for harmony rooted in spiritual commonality.

Moreover, the communication between Joseph and Mary is another pivotal aspect. Their relationship, almost entirely undocumented in words, speaks through actions. Joseph's actions and decisions illustrate his internal dialogue with God, but also his unspoken understanding and respect for Mary. Their marriage is a silent sermon, preaching volumes through the simplicity of lived virtues. This element of non-verbal communication—understanding each other's hearts and intentions without the need for extensive dialogue—can profoundly inspire contemporary marital relationships.

It's essential to recognize Joseph not only as the spouse of Mary but also as someone who played a distinctive role in the history of salvation. This understanding elevates the significance of his marriage to Mary beyond a human commitment to a divine mission. When contemplating their union, one cannot ignore the divine interventions that marked their path—the Annunciation, the dream of the angel, the flight into Egypt. Each event signifies God's active presence in their marital journey, providing a model for marital life fully submitted to divine providence.

Mary's role in this union isn't passive. Despite being chosen as the Mother of God, her consent highlights the importance of mutual acceptance and active participation in marriage. This reciprocation is crucial; it's the merging of two 'yeses' to God's will. Together, they showcase a relationship built on mutual respect and shared mission, where both partners contribute to their divine calling.

For Knights of Columbus who look up to Saint Joseph, emulating this holy marriage encourages not only a personal consecration but also a family consecration. Living out the virtues of humility, obedience, and purity in married life not only enriches the individual but profoundly impacts the family unit and, by extension, society.

Thus, Saint Joseph and the Virgin Mary's marriage exemplifies a divine covenant reflecting God's love for humanity. It teaches that marriage is not merely a union of two bodies but a sacred alliance aimed at achieving divine purposes. By committing to live such virtues, couples can transform their marital life into a sanctifying journey, contributing to their spiritual growth and the glorification of God.

Emulating Saint Joseph in Marital Life lies at the heart of understanding Saint Joseph's multifaceted roles, particularly focusing on his example as a spouse. For many, the figure of Saint Joseph, silent but powerful, epitomizes the ultimate model of marital commitment and virtue. His life offers not just a scriptural lesson but a lived experience that every husband can aspire to embody.

The marriage of Saint Joseph to the Virgin Mary is a divine archetype singled out by God to be the earthly reflection of the Holy Family. It is an instructive model, showcasing marriage as a solemn covenant rooted in mutual love and divine purpose. In an age where marital commitments are often tested and trivialized, Saint Joseph's steadfastness serves as both a beacon and a fortress. To emulate Joseph in marital life is to align oneself with divine will, prioritizing love, respect, and piety in the conjugal relationship.

At the core of Saint Joseph's marital life is his unwavering fidelity. Despite the profound mysteries surrounding Mary's divine maternity, Joseph did not waver; he remained faithful and just. This virtue of fidelity, characterized by unwavering commitment and trust in God's plans, is essential in today's marriages, which frequently face challenges and uncertainties. Joseph's faithfulness invites husbands to cultivate a strong foundation of trust and loyalty, ensuring that the marital bond remains unbroken through trials and tribulations.

Moreover, one cannot overlook the role of humility in the life of Saint Joseph. In the backdrop of his quiet existence lies a powerful humility that accepted God's will without hesitation. His acceptance of Mary and Jesus into his life, despite the potential for societal judgment and personal turmoil, is a testament to his humble obedience. This humility should inspire husbands to prioritize their spouses' spiritual and emotional well-being above personal pride or societal expectations, fostering a home grounded in mutual respect and divine grace.

Joseph's protective nature also extends to his role as a spouse. He was entrusted with safeguarding the Holy Family, guiding them through periods of danger and uncertainty. This protective instinct must be mirrored in every marital relationship, where the husband stands not just as a protector of physical well-being but as a guardian of the spiritual and emotional sanctity of the family. Emulating Joseph involves actively creating an environment where the spiritual practices flourish, where the faith is nurtured, and where the sanctity of marriage is upheld.

One of the profound lessons from Saint Joseph's marital life is his dedication to labor. As a carpenter, Joseph's work was not just a means of sustenance but a form of divine cooperation. His labor was a participation in God's creative work, and by virtue of it, he supported his family. This dedication to labor reminds husbands that their daily work, regardless of how mundane it might seem, is an act of love and service. Emulating Joseph means seeing one's work as intertwined with the divine purpose, contributing to the family's welfare and glorifying God through diligence and integrity.

Furthermore, Saint Joseph exemplifies profound patience and fortitude in his marital life. Throughout his journey, from the Annunciation to the flight into Egypt, his path was fraught with uncertainties and trials. Yet, he remained patient, always trusting in God's plan. Emulating Joseph invites husbands to develop a spirit of patience, understanding that every challenge in marital life is an opportunity for growth and deeper communion with God's will. This patience is not passive but is filled with active trust and hope, guiding couples through their life's journey together.

An often-overlooked aspect of Joseph's marital example is his silent, contemplative nature. In a world filled with noise and distraction, Joseph's silence is profoundly countercultural. His silence was not emptiness but a space filled with God's presence, a contemplative silence that allowed him to listen deeply to God's guidance. Emulating Joseph encourages couples to include moments of silence in their relationship, fostering a contemplative spirit that seeks God's voice amidst the many clamor of daily life.

Finally, the emulation of Saint Joseph in marital life is encapsulated in the virtue of love. His love for Mary was pure, selfless, and wholly oriented towards divine will. This kind of love transcends the mere emotional, reaching the depths of sacrificial commitment and divine purpose. Husbands are called to love their spouses with a selflessness that mirrors Joseph's, willing to lay down one's desires for the greater good of the marital union and the family's spiritual prosperity.

In summation, emulating Saint Joseph in marital life is a profound endeavor that calls for the integration of fidelity, humility, protective care, dedicated labor, patience, contemplative silence, and selfless love. Each of these virtues forms the bedrock of a holy and fulfilling marital life, encouraging husbands to rise to the divine call as Joseph did. By internalizing these virtues, husbands can create a home environment that reflects the sanctity and grace of the Holy Family, drawing ever closer to the divine purpose of their vocation.

Saint Joseph as Father

Saint Joseph exemplifies the quintessence of spiritual fatherhood, guiding us through his silent strength, unwavering faith, and profound commitment to God's will. As the foster father of Jesus, he not only protected and provided for the Holy Family but also embodied the virtues of humility, patience, and obedience. His fatherhood transcends biological ties, serving as a model for spiritual fatherhood in the Catholic tradition. Just as he nurtured and mentored Jesus, we too are called to look to Joseph as a spiritual guide, embracing his exemplary faith to fulfill our own paternal responsibilities. In his quiet yet potent role, Saint Joseph shows that a true father's strength lies in his ability to lead with love, sacrifice, and devotion to both family and God.

Spiritual Fatherhood: Lessons from Saint Joseph provides us unparalleled insights into the nurturing yet firm role that Saint Joseph played in the Holy Family. In this exploration, we are called to see beyond the biological paternity and into a realm where fatherhood transcends the physical, leaving an indelible mark on the spiritual lives entrusted to such care. This form of fatherhood is not bound by blood but is rooted deeply in the divine trust and compassionate leadership that Saint Joseph epitomized.

Saint Joseph stands as a paradigm of spiritual fatherhood, a beacon of what it means to guide, protect, and nurture souls towards holiness. Unlike modern concepts of parental roles which often prioritize achievement and social standing, Saint Joseph's fatherhood is anchored in quiet strength and unwavering faith. His life compels us to re-examine our understanding of fatherhood, pushing us to elevate our expectations towards a divine standard, as opposed to socio-cultural norms.

Saint Joseph's role as a spiritual father is profoundly evident through his interactions with Jesus and Mary. Although the Gospels provide limited details, the narratives that do exist are rich with meaning. In moments of peril, such as the flight into Egypt, we find Saint Joseph acting with decisive protection. We can infer a man whose fatherly love is expressed through action, often silent but never passive. His vigilance taught Jesus not only about a father's protection but also about divine providence. This, in turn, offers today's fathers, both biological and spiritual, an example of how to turn their families towards God's will.

Moreover, Saint Joseph's spiritual fatherhood was honed through his incessant pursuit of righteousness. By obeying divine commands without hesitation, he shows us that true fatherhood involves a relentless dedication to God's directives. This is further illuminated by his unspoken motto of "thy will be done," echoing throughout his life's trials and triumphs. Fathers today are thus called to cultivate a keen discernment of divine will, ensuring that their decisions foster spiritual growth in those they guide.

His diligence in work also speaks volumes about spiritual fatherhood. While many focus on the physical labor Saint Joseph undertook, one must not overlook how his labor nurtured the spiritual environment of the Holy Household. Through his hands, the labor was transformed into a form of worship, imbuing the ordinary with divine significance. Fathers, therefore, are reminded to infuse their daily toil with purpose and devotion, creating a holy space for their families.

Looking at Saint Joseph, we also discover that spiritual fatherhood demands an exceptional degree of quiet strength. His ability to make critical decisions without much fanfare highlights the essence of humility. This humility is profoundly pedagogical; it teaches spiritual fathers to lead without seeking recognition, to be the backdrop against which the souls in their care can flourish. By emulating Saint Joseph's humility, one can cultivate a home where God's voice is paramount, overshadowing personal grandeur.

Another cornerstone of Saint Joseph's fatherhood is his embrace of chastity. This virtue, often misunderstood today, is vital for spiritual fatherhood as it signifies purity and single-hearted devotion. His chaste relationship with Mary, and his protective guardianship of her virginity, radiate the sacredness of his paternal mission. Fathers are invited to examine how they can uphold purity in their own lives and promote it within their families, thereby becoming conduits of God's love and grace.

The protective nature of Saint Joseph's fatherhood cannot be underestimated. His prompt actions in ensuring the safety of Jesus exemplify a father's duty to protect not just the physical well-being, but more importantly, the spiritual welfare of those in his care. In protecting Jesus, Joseph anticipated the dangers and took measures to mitigate them. Fathers today are thus called to be spiritual watchmen, discerning and shielding against modern spiritual perils.

Saint Joseph's spiritual fatherhood also manifests in his capacity to adapt and respond to divine prompts without hesitation. Whether it was abruptly relocating to Egypt or returning to Nazareth, he shows a dynamic responsiveness to God's guiding hand. This flexibility is crucial in spiritual fatherhood, teaching us that while the heavenly goals are steadfast, the earthly paths to them may require attentive and prompt adaptation.

Lastly, the legacy of Saint Joseph's fatherhood is a testament to the enduring influence of a life lived in divine alignment. While societal recognition was minimal in his lifetime, his legacy as a spiritual father is immeasurable within the Church. Today's fathers are thus reminded that their spiritual impact, though often unseen, is eternal and invaluable within God's greater plan. By cultivating a life anchored in righteousness, obedience, and humility, they too can leave a spiritual inheritance of profound worth.

In essence, Saint Joseph's spiritual fatherhood encompasses a profound journey that we are all invited to undertake. His life—marked by protective vigilance, humble strength, pure love, and unwavering obedience—serves as a blueprint for contemporary spiritual fathers. By aligning with the virtues and disciplines that marked Saint Joseph's life, one does not merely fulfill a role but partakes in a divine calling, nurturing souls towards the ultimate fulfillment in God's will.

Thus, understanding and emulating Saint Joseph's spiritual fatherhood is a transformative pathway to divine alignment. May every father, in spirit or in blood, seek to mirror this sanctified example, leading those in their care closer to the heart of God.

Let us now carry these lessons forward, exploring deeper into the expansive roles that Saint Joseph embodies, as we turn to the next sub-section on the Duty of Fatherhood in the Catholic Faith, delving more into the sacred responsibilities entrusted to every father.

The Duty of Fatherhood in the Catholic Faith takes center stage when examining the life and example of Saint Joseph, a paramount figure in the broader context of the Catholic faith. Understanding Saint Joseph's role is more than an academic exercise; it offers tangible guidance for fathers striving to embody Catholic principles in their lives. Saint Joseph's unparalleled blend of humility, strength, and unwavering faith provides a blueprint for fatherhood that transcends time.

In the Catholic tradition, the role of a father is imbued with a sense of divine responsibility. Saint Joseph exemplifies this through his guardianship of Jesus and dedication to Mary. His life serves as an ideal model that reveals the depth and breadth of paternal duty within the framework of faith. The fatherhood seen in Saint Joseph is not merely biological but is grounded in spiritual and moral stewardship. This is paramount in understanding the full scope of what the Catholic Church envisions for fathers.

Saint Joseph's fatherhood encapsulates three core dimensions: protector, provider, and spiritual guide. As protector, Joseph shielded his family from both physical and spiritual dangers. The flight to Egypt, driven by his openness to divine direction through dreams, underscores his role in safeguarding the Holy Family. Fathers today are called to emulate this vigilance, safeguarding the physical and spiritual well-being of their families amidst the myriad challenges of contemporary life.

As a provider, Saint Joseph's labor as a carpenter reflects the dignified work ethic that fathers are encouraged to adopt. This dimension ties fatherhood to the core Catholic teachings on the dignity of labor. By embracing their vocational duties with integrity, fathers can transform ordinary work into an extraordinary offering, reflecting the divine order in their daily tasks. Joseph's hard work, though humble, had profound implications, showing that provision goes beyond material needs to encompass the spiritual sustenance of the family.

The dimension of a spiritual guide is perhaps the most poignant aspect of Saint Joseph's fatherhood. Through his silent yet strong presence, he was the earthly model of obedience to God's will.

Fathers today can find in Joseph a reminder of the importance of leading their families toward a deeper relationship with God. His example teaches that spiritual leadership starts at home, with prayers, sacraments, and a lived example of faith.

In modern contexts, the fullness of fatherhood in the Catholic faith stretches beyond conventional boundaries. It encompasses a life rooted in virtue and sacrificial love. Fathers are called to foster an environment where faith flourishes. By embodying the virtues of Saint Joseph—humility, patience, and unwavering faith—fathers can create homes that mirror the Holy Family's sanctity.

This duty is not without its challenges. In an age where societal norms increasingly diverge from Catholic values, fathers may find themselves swimming against a strong current. Yet, the life of Saint Joseph offers hope and direction. His silent obedience and complete trust in God serve as powerful antidotes to the uncertainties and anxieties that modern fathers face. By turning to Saint Joseph, fathers find a stalwart intercessor who understands the struggles and rewards of fatherhood deeply.

Moreover, Saint Joseph's role as a father underscores the importance of sacramental life. Participation in the sacraments fortifies fathers for their spiritual mission by providing grace and strength. This sacramental life centers on the Eucharist, mirroring Joseph's closeness to Jesus. Fathers are called to embrace the sacraments with devotion not just for their benefit but also as a means to nurture their family's spiritual life.

In an allegorical sense, Saint Joseph's journey is akin to a pilgrimage of faith. Each station along this pilgrimage—whether it be the nativity, the flight to Egypt, or the finding in the temple—reveals a facet of fatherly duty that is relevant today. Fathers, through prayer and reflection, can connect their personal experiences to these pivotal moments in Joseph's life, finding inspiration and insight for their unique journeys.

Therefore, the duty of fatherhood in the Catholic faith, as exemplified by Saint Joseph, calls for a harmonious blend of faith, action, and virtue. The life of Saint Joseph teaches that true fatherhood is an ongoing act of love, sacrifice, and unwavering commitment to guiding one's family toward God. This perspective transforms mundane fatherly tasks into sacred duties that contribute to the spiritual well-being and moral fortitude of the family.

In conclusion, the invitation to consecrate oneself to Saint Joseph is an invitation to reflect on and emulate his exemplary fatherhood. It challenges fathers to aspire to the high standards set by Saint Joseph and to rely on his intercession as they navigate the complexities of modern life. Through this consecration, fathers can find a renewed sense of purpose, inspiration, and divine assistance, ensuring that their fatherhood serves not only their families but also honors the greater glory of God.

Chapter 3: Theology of Consecration

In contemplating the theology of consecration, we engage with a sacred tradition steeped in profound mystery and divine intention. Much like Mary's fiat and Christ's own submission to the Father's will, consecration represents an utter abandonment to God's providence and love. Within this sweeping narrative, Saint Joseph stands as a paragon of obedient faith and silent valor, a figure whose life was singularly dedicated to the sanctity of his mission. To genuinely consecrate oneself, particularly in the context of Roman Catholic piety, one must fully embrace the richness of the Trinitarian mystery: offering our actions and intentions to the Father, in imitation of the Son, and under the guidance of the Holy Spirit. Saint Joseph's unique participation in this divine economy highlights the intertwined roles of protector, provider, and silent witness, making him the ultimate guide for those who seek to live a consecrated life in fidelity and humility. His life embodies a profound theological truth—that true consecration is not a single act but a continual, heartfelt commitment to God's eternal plan.

Consecration to God the Father

Consecration to God the Father forms the bedrock of our spiritual journey, imitating the devotion and trust evident in Saint Joseph's life. It is through such consecration that we acknowledge God the Father as the Alpha and Omega, the ultimate source of love and authority. Saint Joseph, as a model of humility and obedience, exemplifies how to live out this consecration daily. In his silent, steadfast faith and unwavering commitment to God's will, Joseph teaches us that consecrating ourselves to God the Father is not merely a singular act but a continuous, life-encompassing endeavor. This dedication fosters a relationship built on trust, adoration, and the willingness to accept God's divine plan, akin to Joseph's acceptance of his role in the Holy Family. By emulating Joseph, we seek to align our lives more closely with the Heavenly Father, finding in Him our ultimate refuge and strength. It is in this surrender that we grasp the true essence of divine filiation, experiencing a profound father-child relationship that transcends earthly constraints and nurtures our soul's deepest yearnings for divine connection.

Attributes of the Father in Joseph's Life imbue a profound theological richness, revealing facets of God the Father's divine nature through the life of Saint Joseph. Joseph, often depicted in quiet humility and unwavering faith, embodies various characteristics intrinsic to God the Father. These attributes can serve as spiritual guideposts for those seeking to deepen their consecration to God the Father through the example set by Saint Joseph.

One of the core attributes reflected in Joseph's life is his profound sense of obedience. In Scripture, Joseph is repeatedly responsive to divine instructions delivered through dreams. His acceptance of God's call to take Mary as his wife, despite societal norms and potential personal ramifications, showcases an obedience that mirrors God's own command to love and serve above all else. His immediate compliance with the angel's warnings to flee to Egypt further underscores his steadfast commitment to divine will, a reflection of God the Father's immutable command.

Another essential attribute represented in Joseph's life is his protective nature. Just as God the Father is a protector of all creation, Joseph demonstrated an overt commitment to safeguarding his family. His efforts to find shelter in Bethlehem, braving difficult conditions for the birth of Christ, highlight a father's protective instinct. This guardianship mirrors the divine protection God offers to His children, emphasizing trust and reliance on the Father's providential care during times of uncertainty and peril.

Moreover, Joseph's life exudes a steadfast commitment to righteousness, a virtue deeply engrained in the essence of God the Father. Joseph's adherence to Jewish laws and traditions indicates a deep-seated respect for divine ordinance. This righteousness isn't merely a legalistic adherence but rather a demonstration of living in alignment with God's will, a challenge to emulate the sanctity and moral integrity that God the Father represents.

Through the lens of his fatherhood, Joseph's life also exemplifies the nurturing and caring aspects of God the Father. His daily labor as a carpenter, providing for Mary and Jesus, is emblematic of a sacrificial love that reflects divine care. This nurturing spirit shows that fatherhood, while demanding and often sacrificial, is inherently tied to God's own nurturing and sustaining presence in the lives of believers.

Compassion is another divine attribute prevalent in Joseph's life. Throughout various episodes in the Gospel narratives, Joseph's compassionate nature emerges, notably in his initial decision to quietly divorce Mary to shield her from public disgrace. This act of mercy aligns with the compassionate heart of God the Father, who is always ready to forgive and envelop His children in unending grace.

Patience, too, is a remarkable attribute of fatherhood that Joseph radiates. Leading his family through uncertainties, such as the flight into Egypt, required patience and unwavering trust in God's timing. Just as God the Father exhibits boundless patience with humanity, Joseph's life demands a reflection on the virtue of patience as part of one's spiritual journey.

The attribute of wisdom in Joseph's life aligns closely with the omniscient nature of God the Father. His ability to discern and act rightly in critical moments, from accepting Mary as his wife to navigating his family's safety, portrays a wisdom that believers are encouraged to seek. Wisdom, in this context, isn't merely intellectual but deeply spiritual, seeking divine guidance at every juncture.

Additionally, the attribute of silence in Joseph's life embodies a contemplative nature that echoes divine mystery. Though Joseph's spoken words are absent in Scripture, his actions speak volumes. His quiet strength, reflective presence, and meditative disposition point to a deep, abiding connection with God. This silence invites believers to embrace periods of stillness and contemplation, mirroring the Father's voice that often speaks in whispers.

Joseph's life also highlights humility, closely related to God the Father's meekness in approaching humanity through Christ. Despite his critical role, Joseph remained a humble servant, always redirecting glory and honor away from himself and towards God. This humility serves as a poignant reminder for those consecrating themselves to embrace a spirit of humility in their spiritual walk.

Lastly, Joseph's unwavering faith in face of mystery and divine providence reveals an attribute of trustworthiness. By entrusting himself to God's plans, even when they defied human logic, Joseph modeled a relinquishment of self-reliance. This total trust mirrors the Father's trustworthiness, urging the faithful to lean wholly upon divine providence.

In summary, Saint Joseph's life encapsulates numerous attributes of God the Father, each serving as a beacon for those seeking a deeper consecration to the Father. Joseph's obedience, protective nature, righteousness, nurturance, compassion, patience, wisdom, silence, humility, and faith collectively form a tapestry of divine attributes, encouraging the faithful to embody these virtues in their daily lives, aligning closer to the divine nature. Through meditating upon and integrating these attributes, believers can journey towards a more intimate consecration to God the Father, guided by the exemplary life of Saint Joseph.

Consecration to God the Son

In the theology of consecration, dedicating oneself to God the Son is both profound and central to Catholic spirituality. Saint Joseph's exemplary relationship with Jesus offers a profound template for such consecration. Through the Incarnation, Jesus Christ entered the world, God made flesh, and it was under Joseph's nurturing guardianship that Jesus grew in wisdom and stature. Joseph's unwavering faith and obedience stand as a model for embracing and serving God the Son with genuine devotion. This consecration involves aligning one's life with the teachings and sacrifice of Christ, reflecting His love, humility, and service. As we commit our existence to Him, we recognize Joseph's unique role in Salvation History and seek to emulate his steadfast dedication. Therefore, consecration to God the Son becomes not merely an act of devotion but a transformative journey towards embodying the virtues exemplified in the Holy Family.

The Incarnation and Joseph's Role illuminates a profound aspect of the divinely orchestrated plan of salvation, particularly accentuating Joseph's participation in the mystery of the Word becoming flesh. Embedded within the larger framework of "Theology of Consecration" and deeply linked to "Consecration to God the Son," this section explores how Joseph's unique role in the Incarnation exemplifies virtues essential for any consecrated life, particularly for members of the Knights of Columbus. Joseph's guardianship and his unwavering faith symbolize ultimate surrender to the divine will, a perfect alignment with the life and mission of Jesus Christ.

Joseph's role in the Incarnation extends beyond mere historical context; it signifies an archetype for spiritual fatherhood and divine stewardship. Sacred Scripture recounts how Joseph, a humble carpenter, was chosen by God to protect and nurture Jesus Christ. This divine election underscores Joseph's unparalleled participation in the mystery of salvation. Through his acceptance, Joseph becomes not only a guardian of the Holy Family but also a pivotal figure in God's divine plan. He embodies the spirit of consecration by integrating his daily labors and struggles into a life that ultimately serves God's redemptive work.

At the announcement of Mary's miraculous conception, Joseph's initial reaction was one of quiet discernment. The Gospel of Matthew (1:18-25) portrays Joseph as a "righteous man," reflecting his inner turmoil yet deep faith. Faced with what seemed an insurmountable crisis, he chose to listen to the angelic message and take Mary as his wife. This decision reveals his readiness to consecrate himself entirely to the will of God. For the Knights of Columbus, Joseph stands as a model of trusting patience and discerning obedience, essential traits for anyone pledging their life to God's service.

Moreover, Joseph's silent strength during the journey to Bethlehem, the birth of Jesus in a humble manger, and the flight into Egypt embodies the virtues of humility, resilience, and protective care. His actions were imbued with sanctity, illustrating a life wholly offered in service to the Incarnate Word. His sacrifices and hardships speak to a level of divine consecration that goes beyond words, serving as a living testament to the demands and rewards of being fully committed to God's plan.

The significance of Joseph's silence is not to be overlooked. His actions spoke louder than words, revealing a profound depth of faith and commitment. Unlike many Biblical figures, Joseph does not have any spoken lines recorded in Scripture. This silence itself becomes a powerful symbol of his consecrated life. It invites us to contemplate the holiness found in everyday duties and the courage required to follow God's will without the need for human recognition or accolade. In Joseph's silent obedience, there lies a call for the Knights of Columbus to embrace a life of action driven by faith.

Furthermore, Joseph's role in the Incarnation emphasizes the sanctification of work and daily toil. As a carpenter, he provided for Jesus and Mary through his labor. This example teaches us that holiness can be achieved within the context of ordinary life through diligence, integrity, and dedication. For the Knights of Columbus, who balance family obligations with their religious commitments, Joseph's life serves as a beacon, showcasing that one's trade, when carried out faithfully, contributes to the divine economy of salvation.

Joseph's role in the early life of Jesus also underscores the importance of spiritual fatherhood. By accepting Jesus as his son, Joseph showed profound faith and trust in God's promise. He mentored Jesus, instructed him in the trade of carpentry, and protected him from danger. This paternal dimension of Joseph's role further elucidates the sacrificial love required in the life of those consecrated to God. The Knights of Columbus, who often serve as spiritual leaders within their families and communities, can look to Joseph as an exemplar of fatherly guidance intertwined with divine mission.

In light of the Incarnation, Joseph's guardianship of Jesus is more than a protective duty; it reflects a deeper theological reality. It illustrates the collaborative nature of divine-human partnership in the history of salvation. By entrusting His Son to Joseph, God dignified human fatherhood and sanctified it as a vehicle for divine grace. The Knights of Columbus, consecrating themselves to God the Son, are invited to participate in this divine-human synergy by embodying virtues of courage, humility, and unwavering devotion in their daily lives.

Joseph's role continues to provide rich theological insights into the unitary nature of the Holy Family, an earthly representation of the heavenly Trinity. His unwavering commitment to Mary and Jesus, despite the trials they faced, serves as a living icon of familial love rooted in divine will. It is an invitation for the Knights to nurture their families with the same sacrificial love and steadfastness, grounded in faith and devoted to God's plan.

Thus, "The Incarnation and Joseph's Role" becomes not only a historical event but a living, breathing model of consecration alive in the Knight's every action. Each gesture of Joseph's life was imbued with divine purpose, reflecting a heart wholly devoted to God's Word made flesh. In modeling their lives after Joseph, the Knights find a path to deeper union with God through the diligent execution of daily tasks, unyielding faith amidst trials, and a life perpetually oriented towards divine service.

In conclusion, Joseph's participation in the mystery of the Incarnation is a luminous example of how ordinary life, when oriented towards God, can become extraordinary. His unwavering faith, silent strength, and humble service reveal the profound depths of consecration to God the Son. This journey invites each member of the Knights of Columbus to embrace a life where every action, no matter how mundane, is offered as a sacrifice of love to the divine. By consecrating themselves in the spirit of Saint Joseph, they not only honor the guardian of Jesus but also activate their own role in God's salvific plan, embodying the virtues and faith that define a life consecrated to Christ.

Consecration to God the Holy Spirit

In the sacred act of consecrating oneself to God the Holy Spirit, one embarks on a pilgrimage of divine intimacy and spiritual illumination. The Holy Spirit, who guided Saint Joseph with celestial wisdom, beckons us to surrender our will, transforming every action into a testament of faith and divine love. This consecration is not a mere ritual but a heartfelt embrace of the Spirit's whispering call, echoing through the epochs of sacred scripture and the annals of the Church. By seeking the Holy Spirit's guidance, the consecrated soul imitates Saint Joseph in his silent but steadfast obedience, allowing the breath of God to animate mundane tasks into sacraments of grace. As Knights of Columbus, this consecration asks us to harness the Spirit's gifts—wisdom, understanding, and fortitude—to become vessels of His divine will, living lives that reflect the consummate unity of the Father, the Son, and the Holy Spirit. Through this transformative act, the faithful are drawn into deeper communion with God, emblematic of Saint Joseph's own unwavering fidelity and sanctity.

The Spirit's Guidance in Saint Joseph's Actions permeates every facet of his life, offering a profound and deeply rooted model for consecration to God the Holy Spirit. To fully understand the sanctity and role of Saint Joseph, we must delve into the mysterious yet intimate relationship he held with the Holy Spirit, guiding his actions with divine providence and wisdom. This spiritual synergy is what makes his life a blueprint for those seeking to commit themselves fully to God's will through the Holy Spirit.

Saint Joseph, often depicted as a humble carpenter, was far more than meets the eye. His simplicity and devotion were manifestations of his complete surrender to the Holy Spirit's guidance. One of the clearest examples of this divine inspiration is Joseph's reaction to Mary's unexpected pregnancy. It is in these moments of inner turmoil that the angel's visitation becomes pivotal—not merely as an event but as a profound testament to how the Holy Spirit actively directed his choices. The Spirit's whisper gave him the strength to trust in God's plan, embracing Mary and her divine mission without hesitation.

In the quiet town of Nazareth, Joseph's daily acts of labor were not merely tasks but prayers in motion, indicating a life that's continuously yielding to the Spirit's promptings. His willingness to labor diligently not only provided for the Holy Family but also illustrated the Holy Spirit's role in sanctifying even the most mundane of tasks. In Saint Joseph's hands, the humblest pieces of wood transcended their earthly form, becoming symbols of divine craftsmanship and sanctified human effort.

Moreover, the journey to Bethlehem, the flight into Egypt, and the return to Nazareth are not just geographical migrations but spiritual journeys paved through the Holy Spirit's guidance. Each step Joseph took was a testament to his unwavering faith and the Spirit's unyielding prompt. These journeys were filled with danger, uncertainty, and hardships, yet Joseph moved forward undeterred. To truly understand these decisions, one must acknowledge the Spirit's invisible hand guiding him along the treacherous paths, ensuring the protection and fulfillment of God's plan.

Joseph's patience and trust during these journeys showed a man who did not merely follow orders but entered into a profound dialogue with God through the Holy Spirit. This dialogue was not marked by grand revelations but by a quiet, steady assurance that he was part of a divine plan much larger than himself. The Holy Spirit's guidance created a path that allowed Joseph to lead, protect, and nurture the very embodiment of divine love, the Christ child, and his mother, Mary.

During the hidden years at Nazareth, Joseph continued to act under the Spirit's influence. His role as Jesus' earthly father was steeped in spiritual guidance that showcased extraordinary prudence and foresight. Teaching Jesus the skills of carpentry, Joseph honored the Holy Spirit's influence by nurturing both the human and divine aspects of Jesus' life. This sacred tutelage emphasizes that Joseph's actions, although seemingly ordinary, were invested with divine intention, reflecting the Holy Spirit's sanctifying power at every moment.

Joseph's silence in the scriptures speaks volumes of his relationship with the Holy Spirit. In a world where actions often speak louder than words, Joseph's choices, and deeds echo the Spirit's subtle yet powerful presence. His ability to listen, discern, and act upon God's will without seeking personal glory or recognition is an eloquent testament to the profound influence of the Holy Spirit. Joseph's silence is a sanctified space where the Spirit's guidance becomes most apparent, encouraging us to seek and cultivate that same inner stillness in our lives.

One must also consider Joseph's exemplary obedience to the Holy Spirit's will. Obedience, rooted in trust and humility, is perhaps the clearest sign of divine guidance in one's life. Joseph displayed perfect obedience, not as a burden but as a willing, joyful submission to God's plan. Each act of compliance—from his acceptance of Mary to his guardianship over Jesus—reveals a profound synthesis of human freewill and divine orchestration, meticulously curated by the Holy Spirit.

Reflecting on Saint Joseph's actions provides a roadmap for our consecration to the Holy Spirit. By observing the Spirit's dynamic interplay in Joseph's life, we learn that true consecration goes beyond mere devotion; it requires an active, responsive heart aligned with the Spirit's whispers. It invites us into a deeper participation in the divine will, modeling our lives after a man who, though carved in the ordinary, was shaped by the extraordinary influence of the Holy Spirit.

Finally, Saint Joseph's legacy of actions under the Spirit's guidance calls us to emulate his faith. In our contemporary setting, where distractions abound, committing ourselves wholly to the Holy Spirit demands intentionality and perseverance. Like Saint Joseph, we are invited to embrace a life of discernment, where each decision, no matter how small, is infused with prayerful consideration and submission to divine guidance. This alignment transforms our daily walk into a spiritual pilgrimage, drawing us ever closer to the heart of God.

The Spirit's Guidance in Saint Joseph's Actions provides an in-depth exploration of how the Holy Spirit can lead us into a fuller, richer experience of God's plan. Through the lens of Joseph's life, we see the beauty of a consecrated life, illuminated by the Spirit's ceaseless guidance, and are encouraged to surrender our hearts and actions to the same divine influence.

Chapter 4: Pedagogical Aspects of Living the Divine Will

In the journey of consecration, embracing the Divine Will serves as an enduring guidepost, shaping not only the spiritual but also the practical dimensions of life. It necessitates a profound alignment of one's actions, thoughts, and intentions with the eternal wisdom of God. This harmonious synchrony is not merely an exercise in dutiful compliance but a transformative pedagogy, embedding divine precepts into the fabric of daily existence. By living the Divine Will, believers engage in a dynamic relationship with God, where learning and living converge, mirroring Saint Joseph's silent yet potent adherence to God's commands. This convergence calls for a vigilant discernment, continuously seeking God's intentions through prayer, contemplation, and active participation in the sacraments. Saint Joseph's life exemplifies this pedagogical process; his humble obedience illuminates the path of instructive faith, encouraging the integration of divine truths within the ordinary and extraordinary facets of life. Thus, living the Divine Will becomes a lived theology that instructs and sanctifies, positioning the believer as both a student and a testament to God's boundless wisdom.

Understanding the Divine Will

Understanding the Divine Will is foundational to living a life consecrated to Saint Joseph. The Divine Will, in its most profound sense, is God's loving plan for humanity, intricately woven into each of our lives. To grasp its depth, one must first recognize the interplay between divine sovereignty and human freedom. It's akin to music; God composes the symphony, but we, as individual instruments, must faithfully follow the score.

Our understanding of the Divine Will is not merely an intellectual exercise but a lived experience. It invites a heart-tuned receptivity, a dynamic surrender that manifests through action. Saint Joseph's life exemplifies this beautifully. Though scripture provides us sparse details about his words, his actions speak volumes. By embracing his role as protector, worker, spouse, and father, Joseph aligned himself seamlessly with God's will.

In his silent acceptance and obedient heart, Joseph demonstrated unwavering trust in God's plan. When the angel appeared to him in a dream and commanded him to take Mary as his wife, Joseph did not hesitate. His actions were not passive; they were a vibrant testament to his fidelity and discernment. In this regard, Joseph serves as a pedagogue, teaching us how to attune our lives to the Divine Will.

Moreover, understanding the Divine Will requires us to navigate life's uncertainties with faith. Consider the flight into Egypt—an urgent and perilous journey commanded by divine instruction. Joseph's swift compliance, without questioning the peril or the discomfort it entailed, reflected his deep trust in God's providence. Here, the Divine Will might not always align with human logic or comfort, yet it is invariably aimed at a greater good.

The Divine Will transcends mere personal desires and ambitions. It calls us to a higher purpose and requires the sacrifice of our understanding and comfort. Saint Joseph's example underscores the need for humility and subservience. This divine alignment transforms our actions from mundane to sublime, from ordinary to sacramental. Living the Divine Will thus becomes a sacred endeavor, where each act, no matter how humble, carries eternal significance.

To deepen our understanding, we must engage in prayerful reflection and study of the scriptures. The Word of God is replete with instances illustrating the harmony between divine instruction and human execution. In Joseph's life, both the Old and New Testaments converge revealing the typology of a man in complete harmony with divine imperatives. In our study, we glean insights not only through his direct actions but also in the way he nurtured and protected the Holy Family, which symbolizes the Church.

Yet, understanding the Divine Will is not confined to scriptural interpretation alone; it extends to the Church's teachings and traditions. The Magisterium provides a rich tapestry of insights into how saints, theologians, and scholars have interpreted and lived the Divine Will over centuries. The Catechism, for instance, can be a guiding tool, offering concrete principles on aligning one's life with God's desires.

Analogically, the relationship between Divine Will and human cooperation can be likened to the craftsman and his tools. A tool, no matter how perfected, accomplishes nothing of its own accord. It is the craftsman's guidance, precision, and purpose that bring forth the masterpiece. In this analogy, we are the tools, Saint Joseph the exemplar craftsman, and God the ultimate artist directing us towards the fulfillment of His divine masterpiece.

Discernment plays a crucial role in understanding the Divine Will. It involves a spiritual sensitivity, an attunement to the divine promptings often referred to as the "still small voice." Discernment is not simply recognizing divine signs but responding with trust and dedication. Saint Joseph's life illustrates continuous discernment—whether it was deciding to secretly divorce Mary, heeding the angel's message in a dream, or settling in Nazareth after the exile. Each step was a conscious, faith-driven decision aligning with divine intent.

Furthermore, theologians highlight the importance of community in comprehending the Divine Will. The Church, as the Body of Christ, often channels God's directives through communal discernment. In Joseph's context, his decisions impacted not just his immediate family but the unfolding of salvation history. Thus, our individual and collective discernment can never be isolated; it is intrinsically linked to the broader ecclesial context. The Knights of Columbus, with their charisms of fraternity and service, embody this communal response to Divine Will.

But understanding extends beyond intellectual assimilation; it encompasses the transformative action spurred by faith. Consider the Knights of Columbus who vow to live according to the virtues exemplified by Saint Joseph. They must transcend mere admiration of Joseph's life to embodying his virtues in concrete actions through charitable works, defending the faith, and promoting familial and societal wellbeing.

Lastly, the journey towards understanding the Divine Will is perpetual. It is a lifelong pilgrimage marked by growth in virtue, deepening prayer, and a faith that remains unwavering amidst trials. The Divine Will is, paradoxically, both a mystery and a revelation. Through the lens of Saint Joseph, we find a tangible model of how to navigate this pilgrimage with integrity, courage, and unwavering trust in God's providential care.

In sum, "Understanding the Divine Will" is an invitation to a profound, transformative relationship with God. It calls us to follow Saint Joseph's lead—embracing divine promptings with faith, acting with unwavering obedience, and living with a heart attuned to God's loving plan. Through the intertwining of faith, action, and the grace of discernment, we journey ever closer to the heart of God's will, making our lives a testament to His eternal love and purpose.

Acting in Accordance with the Divine Will

Gazing upon the life of Saint Joseph, one finds a paragon of alignment with the Divine Will. His every action and decision resonate with the echo of a higher purpose, an unwavering commitment to the divine plan set forth by God. In understanding and emulating Saint Joseph, we properly appreciate what it means to act in accordance with the Divine Will.

To begin, we must grasp the significance of Divine Will in Catholic theology. It is not merely a set of commandments or an abstract ideal. Rather, it is God's ultimate plan for humanity, woven into the fabric of creation since time immemorial. Saint Joseph's life lays bare this truth, displaying an unwavering cohesion with God's intentions. His responses to angelic messages and his actions in safeguarding the Holy Family exemplify obedience to Divine Will.

Acting in accordance with the Divine Will demands conscious discernment and unwavering trust in God. It requires surrendering personal desires and ambitions to embrace a larger divine purpose. Saint Joseph exemplifies this beautifully. In moments of uncertainty, like when he was unsure about taking Mary as his wife, Joseph demonstrates that true alignment with the Divine Will often involves a leap of faith, trusting in the guidance and providence of God.

In a practical sense, adherence to Divine Will involves regular prayer, meditation, and spiritual discernment. Just as Joseph received divine messages through dreams and angelic visitation, we, too, must cultivate a sensitivity to divine promptings. This sensitivity can only be developed through a consistent spiritual practice that tunes our hearts and minds to God's voice.

Furthermore, acting in accordance with God's Will requires humility and a willingness to be led. Saint Joseph's humility is evident in his silent yet formidable presence in the Gospels. His actions speak louder than any recorded words, illustrating that humility is not passive but an active, courageous engagement in God's plan. Humility allows the heart to be molded by Divine Will, transforming personal ambitions into divine aspirations.

There's an aspect of active participation in living out the Divine Will. Saint Joseph's labor as a carpenter, his dedication to providing for his family, and his protective stance over Mary and Jesus define a life of sacred action. Each nail he hammered, every piece of wood he shaped, was an extension of his divine mandate. Likewise, Acts in daily life, no matter how mundane, can serve as conduits of Divine Will when performed with devotion and intentionality.

Living in accordance with God's Will calls for moral and ethical consistency. Joseph's decisions were rooted in righteousness and fidelity to Jewish Law, reflecting a deep commitment to God's moral order. This moral clarity provided Joseph with a solid foundation upon which he could discern and enact the Divine Will. His life calls us to the same moral integrity, urging us to align our ethical decisions with divine wisdom.

The virtue of patience is another cornerstone of acting in accord with God's will, as evidenced in Joseph's response to divine directives. His patience amidst uncertainty—whether waiting for the safe return from Egypt or raising the Son of God—illustrates how patience aligns us more closely with Divine Will. Patience allows God's plan to unfold in its own time, reminding us that rushing God's timing often leads to misalignment with His ultimate purpose.

Moreover, trust in Divine Providence is indispensable. Joseph's trust in God's provision—whether for guidance, sustenance, or protection—exemplifies the depth of reliance required to act in accordance with God's Will. It teaches us that Divine Will is often carried out through the dependencies and contingencies of life, requiring us to trust that God's provision will never fail us, even in our darkest hours.

An integral part of living the Divine Will is service to others. Saint Joseph's life was characterized by selfless service to his family and his community. His example underscores the understanding that acting according to God's Will often involves serving others, reflecting Christ's love and compassion through actions. This service, in turn, brings us closer to the heart of God's purpose for our lives.

Furthermore, the contemplative aspect of Joseph's life teaches us about the necessity of silence and reflection in discernment. His silent strength and contemplative nature allowed him to hear God's voice clearly. In today's fast-paced world, creating moments of silence and reflection is crucial for discerning and aligning with Divine Will. These practices allow our hearts to be attuned to God's still, small voice guiding us through life.

Moreover, the alignment with the Divine Will is deeply interwoven with sacramental life. Saint Joseph's life was a living sacrament, an outward sign of inward grace. Participation in the sacraments—especially the Eucharist and Reconciliation—fortifies our ability to align our actions with God's Will. These sacraments nourish us with divine grace, essential for sustaining a life dedicated to God.

And finally, one must not overlook the importance of community in discerning and acting in Divine Will. Saint Joseph lived within a community of faith, drawing strength and support from it. As modern-day followers of Christ, our community of faith—the Church—provides guidance, accountability, and encouragement. It reminds us that we are not solitary agents but part of a divine tapestry, each thread contributing to the whole.

In sum, acting in accordance with the Divine Will encompasses prayerful discernment, ethical consistency, humility, patience, trust in Divine Providence, service to others, silence and reflection, sacramental life, and community involvement. Saint Joseph's life is a profound testament to these principles. By learning from his example, we, too, can aspire to align our lives with the Divine Will, fostering a deeper union with God and advancing His Kingdom on Earth.

Chapter 5: The Duty of Religion

The duty of religion, dear brothers and sisters, acts as the sacred bridge uniting the divine and mundane aspects of human existence. To truly consecrate oneself to Saint Joseph, one must immerse in practices of devout piety that resonate beyond the walls of the church, seeping into the very fiber of daily life. Following in Saint Joseph's humble footsteps, embracing prayer, and engaging in sacramental life are not merely obligations but profound expressions of our love for God. The holy patriarch, whose earthly toil was sanctified by his unwavering faith, teaches us that religion is not an isolated segment of life but the lifeblood that courses through every action, every moment. Our vocation thus is to weave religious devotion seamlessly into our daily routines, transforming ordinary tasks into sacred offerings. This duty, illuminated by Saint Joseph's example, becomes our compass, guiding us toward a life intertwined with divine purpose and anchored in unwavering faith.

Engaging in Devout Practices

Engaging in devout practices is paramount to the spiritual formation of any Knight of Columbus aspiring for deeper communion with Saint Joseph. Devout practices are not mere ritualistic acts performed out of obligation but are intentional and heartfelt actions that align our hearts, minds, and souls with the divine will. Through these practices, we find ourselves drawn closer to God's grace, continuously reminded of our purpose and duty in the grand tapestry of the Catholic faith.

Saint Joseph, in his immaculate obedience and humility, offers an exemplary model for devout practices. His life was marked by unwavering devotion to God's will. From his laborious days as a carpenter to his dutiful care for the Holy Family, Joseph's every action was a testimony to his intense spiritual commitment. By emulating Joseph, one can transform mundane activities into spiritual offerings, thus sanctifying daily life.

One cannot overstate the importance of prayer in engaging in devout practices. Prayer is the lifeline that connects the soul to the Divine. Incorporating regular, structured prayer sessions helps cultivate a sense of discipline and reverence. The Liturgy of the Hours, the Rosary, and the daily recitation of prayers dedicated to Saint Joseph are all potent tools for this purpose. Praying at designated times throughout the day—morning, noon, and night—creates a rhythm that continually draws the faithful into God's presence, encouraging a ceaseless dialogue with the Creator.

Incorporating the sacraments into our lives intensifies our spiritual journey. Frequent participation in the Eucharist and regular confession are indispensable. The Eucharist, being the source and summit of Christian life, nourishes the soul and fortifies the spirit. Confession, on the other hand, offers a cleansing of the soul, absolving sins, and renewing our divine commitment. Saint Joseph, although sinless by the grace of his proximity to Jesus and Mary, demonstrates utter submissiveness to the sacrosanct traditions and their transformative powers.

The practice of meditative reading, also known as lectio divina, enriches our devotion. Immersing oneself in the sacred scriptures allows for a personal encounter with God's word. The life of Saint Joseph, though sparingly detailed in the scriptures, bursts into fullness through meditative reading. Reflecting on the passages from Matthew and Luke that mention Joseph, we see beyond the written words and gain profound insights into his virtues and divine mission.

Embracing a life of simplicity, as Saint Joseph did, is another vital practice. Simplicity manifests not only in material detachment but also in the purity of heart and intention. In a world obsessed with material success and superficial accolades, striving for a life of humility and service becomes a radical act of faith. Joseph's life, though outwardly simple, was imbued with divine richness. Imitating his virtues of humility, obedience, and quiet strength, we align ourselves with the divine will and predispose our hearts to receive grace.

Fasting and abstinence present age-old practices that fortify spiritual discipline. These acts of self-denial make room for God's grace to flourish within us. In moments of abstinence, whether from food, luxuries, or personal comforts, we echo Christ's suffering, align ourselves with His sacrifice, and purify our spirits. Saint Joseph, known for his temperate and chaste life, exemplifies the spiritual benefits derived from such practices.

Almsgiving, too, is a cornerstone of devout practice. By sharing our resources with those in need, we emulate the generous spirit of Saint Joseph. Almsgiving is an antidote to greed and materialism, reinforcing our commitment to the teachings of Christ. Saint Joseph's protection and provision for the Holy Family demonstrate how our own sacrifices can fortify and nurture those around us. The very act of giving joyfully acknowledges our trust in divine providence, aware that all we have ultimately belongs to God.

Moreover, engaging in community worship plays a vital role in our spiritual journey. Participating in Mass, communal prayers, and religious gatherings strengthens the bonds within the faith community. Saint Joseph, a devout Jew, observed religious traditions with fidelity, offering us a blueprint for living out our faith in communion with others. The Knights of Columbus, driven by their united mission, can fortify their spiritual lives through frequent and collective prayers, ensuring every member feels connected to a larger purpose.

Learning from the saints is another advantageous practice. The liturgical calendar offers numerous opportunities to reflect upon the lives of those who have walked this path of righteousness before us. Saint Joseph's feast days, March 19th and May 1st, should be profoundly observed with special prayers, Masses, and devotions. These moments of veneration help deepen our understanding of his role and inspire us to emulate his virtues daily.

In navigating contemporary challenges, keeping a steadfast focus on spiritual practices that Saint Joseph exemplified offers invaluable guidance. Balancing vocational responsibilities, familial duties, and spiritual commitments might seem formidable, yet Joseph's life assures us that it is plausible. His unwavering faith, resilience in adversities, and unflinching devotion to his divine mission offer practical insights into living out one's faith amidst modern complexities.

Ultimately, engaging in devout practices is about orchestrating the entirety of our lives into a symphony of worship. Like Saint Joseph, whose every act was an ode to divine will, our actions, sacrifices, and prayers should coalesce into a harmonious offering that continually glorifies God. As Knights of Columbus, dedicating ourselves to such practices not only draws us nearer to Saint Joseph but also fortifies the very essence of our existence and mission in this world.

This engagement transforms our journey of faith from mere observance to vibrant, dynamic, and profound sainthood. The key is consistency, sincerity, and an unwavering commitment to pursuing holiness through these devout practices, inspired by the life and virtues of Saint Joseph.

Integrating Religion into Daily Life

Integrating religion into daily life requires more than mere ritual or tradition. It is the embodiment of faith in every action, decision, and moment we encounter. As Knights of Columbus, our obligation to Saint Joseph and to our faith must permeate all facets of our lives, transforming the mundane into the sacred.

Saint Joseph, a humble carpenter from Nazareth, exemplifies this integration through his unwavering faith and steadfast devotion. He did not live a segmented life, dividing the sacred from the secular. Everything he did—whether working with his hands, caring for his family, or adhering to divine instructions—was imbued with a deep sense of religious duty. His life serves as a powerful lesson for all of us who aspire to live holistically under the guidance of our faith.

One of the foremost ways to integrate religion into daily life is through the practice of constant prayer. Not just formal prayers, but also brief moments of silent communication with God throughout the day can transform our perspectives. For instance, invoking Saint Joseph before starting a work task can sanctify even the most routine activities. By doing this, we acknowledge that every action, no matter how small, can be an offering to God.

Another important aspect is living by the virtues exemplified by Saint Joseph. Patience, humility, and obedience are not confined to spiritual exercises; they should manifest in how we interact with our coworkers, treat our families, and face personal challenges. Imagine a working day marked by the humility and diligence of Saint Joseph, handling not only professional responsibilities with grace but also offering support and understanding to colleagues. In doing so, we bring the principles of our faith into every interaction, every decision.

Family life presents a unique opportunity for religious integration, and Saint Joseph's role as the head of the Holy Family provides a perfect model. Balancing parental duties with spiritual leadership, he shows that fatherhood is both a vocation and a divine mission. Teaching children about the faith, involving them in acts of charity, and setting an example through one's own devout practices help cultivate a household where religion is a natural part of daily life.

Furthermore, the observance of the sacraments is crucial. Participating in the Eucharist, regularly engaging in the Sacrament of Reconciliation, and encouraging a family prayer routine are not just acts of piety but are fundamental ways to integrate faith seamlessly into our daily rhythm. These practices align our lives closely with the divine will and allow us to draw spiritual strength for our earthly duties.

The work environment too offers a myriad of opportunities for religious integration. Saint Joseph, renowned as a worker, demonstrates how labor can be an act of worship when done with the right disposition. Whether it is the honesty of our dealings, the quality of our work, or the respect we show to colleagues, infusing our professional life with Christian values creates an atmosphere where faith and work coexist harmoniously.

It is also vital to integrate social justice and ethical principles derived from our faith into our daily actions. This involves not just adhering to doctrine but actively seeking out ways to live it. Volunteering for community service, advocating for the marginalized, and treating everyone with the dignity they deserve reflect a life that is deeply intertwined with religious beliefs. Saint Joseph, as the protector of the Holy Family, embodies this protective spirit, urging us to look after the most vulnerable in our society.

Take, for example, the small act of sharing a meal. By saying grace, offering a prayer for those in need, and perhaps even inviting someone less fortunate to join you, a common activity is transformed into an act of grace and community. These little acts, when performed with intention, bring the sacred into our everyday routines.

Communal activities also provide fertile ground for the integration of religion. Being active in the parish, joining prayer groups, or participating in the Knights of Columbus' charitable endeavors can further cement this connection. These activities not only strengthen our personal faith but also contribute to the broader mission of the Church, turning individual acts of devotion into collective expressions of our shared beliefs.

Furthermore, fostering a mindset of gratitude can significantly impact how we see our daily tasks. By recognizing God's hand in all things and expressing thankfulness for both blessings and challenges, we create an ongoing dialogue with the divine. This shift in perspective allows us to see each moment as an opportunity for spiritual growth.

Liturgical seasons provide another framework for integrating religion into daily life. The rhythm of Advent, Christmas, Lent, and Easter offers a cyclical pattern of reflection, celebration, penance, and renewal. By aligning our personal practices with these seasons, we find natural pauses to deepen our devotion and reflect on our spiritual journey.

Finally, contemplation should not be dismissed as a lofty ideal impractical for daily life. Short periods of quiet reflection can recalibrate our thoughts and intentions, aligning them more closely with divine will. Whether it is through lectio divina, silent adoration, or simply a few moments of peace in a busy day, contemplation adds a layer of depth to our daily religious practice.

To integrate religion into daily life fully, one must see every act as an opportunity to glorify God and seek His will, much like Saint Joseph did. This integration is not a series of disjointed actions, but a cohesive lifestyle where faith naturally informs every aspect of our existence. For Knights of Columbus, this path isn't just a recommendation but a solemn duty, echoing the profound devotion of Saint Joseph himself.

Chapter 6: Observing All Commandments

In the journey toward consecration to Saint Joseph, observing all commandments emerges as not only a duty but as a profound spiritual practice, anchored in both the Old and the New Testaments. Saint Joseph, though described succinctly in the Scriptures, embodies a profound reverence and adherence to God's commandments. His life, a living testament to humility and unwavering obedience, offers a guidepost for contemporary believers striving to align their actions with divine law. To truly embody Saint Joseph's example, one must understand that the commandments are more than rules; they are divinely endowed principles that ensure a harmonious relationship with God and others. As Knights of Columbus, the call to observe these commandments gains even more significance when considering the societal roles and responsibilities one undertakes. The integration of these divine laws into daily life not only fosters personal holiness but also strengthens the collective spiritual fabric of the community. Therefore, in emulating Saint Joseph's silent, steadfast faithfulness, we are encouraged to examine and realign our modern lives continually, ensuring every action, word, and thought reflects the sanctity expected by the commandments. This observance is not a burdensome obligation but a joyful embrace of a life devoted entirely to God's will, echoing Saint Joseph's exemplary path.

The Ten Commandments and Saint Joseph's Example

When reflecting upon the Ten Commandments, it becomes clear how they serve not merely as laws but as divine expectations that shape and guide the life of every Catholic. Saint Joseph, in his quiet yet powerful example, embodies these commandments impeccably. As we consecrate ourselves to Saint Joseph, understanding how he manifests the observance of these divine laws is paramount.

The First Commandment calls us to honor God above all else. Saint Joseph's entire life was a testament to this absolute reverence. From the moment he accepted the angel's message regarding Mary's divine conception, Joseph displayed unwavering faith. His silent obedience was a continual act of worship, showing that true adoration of God manifests in humble compliance with His will. He reminds us that putting God first means listening and acting upon His word, even when it challenges our understanding.

Next, we consider the Second Commandment, which instructs us not to take the Lord's name in vain. Saint Joseph, ever respectful and dignified, guarded the sanctity of God's name through his actions. His life, dedicated to supporting Jesus and Mary, was a constant prayer in itself. Through his work and protection of the Holy Family, Joseph exemplified the deep respect and sacredness due to God's name and identity.

The Third Commandment commands us to keep the Sabbath day holy. Joseph, as a devout Jew, would have observed the Sabbath with diligence. Yet, his entire life can be seen as a form of keeping the Sabbath holy. By creating a home where Jesus could grow in wisdom and grace, Joseph ensured that every day was infused with the sacred, turning ordinary moments into continuous acts of sanctification. This invites us to not only observe our holy days but to bring that sanctity into our daily lives.

The Fourth Commandment speaks of honoring one's father and mother. Although Joseph was the earthly guardian of Jesus, he shows profound respect and care for Mary, his spouse. His deference to her role and his protection of her dignity highlight the mutual respect central to family life. Joseph's example teaches us that honoring our parents involves respect, care, and support, contributing to a loving and stable family dynamic.

The Fifth Commandment, "Thou shalt not kill," is embodied by Joseph through his protective nature. By fleeing to Egypt to save Jesus from Herod's massacre, Joseph did everything in his power to protect life. He acts as a model for us to respect and safeguard life in all its stages, reminding us of the proactive steps we can take to defend life against any form of harm.

The Sixth Commandment, which concerns the sanctity of marriage and fidelity, can be illuminated through Joseph's chaste marriage to Mary. Despite the unique circumstances surrounding Jesus' birth, Joseph remained wholly committed and faithful. His life exemplified the purity and steadfastness required in marital relationships. Joseph calls us to honor our spouses wholeheartedly, to build relationships founded on trust and fidelity.

Seventh, the commandment, "Thou shalt not steal," extends beyond the mere act of taking someone else's possessions. Saint Joseph exemplifies this through his honesty and integrity as a carpenter. He earned his livelihood through hard work and dedication, never taking what was not his. In a world full of shortcuts and temptations, Joseph's life urges us to be honest in all our dealings, embodying fairness and justice.

The Eighth Commandment instructs us not to bear false witness. Joseph's life was marked by truth and transparency. Whether dealing with family, neighbors, or God, he conducted himself with utter honesty. His straightforwardness stands as a testament to the importance of living in truth, avoiding deceit and misrepresentation in every aspect of our lives.

The Ninth Commandment calls for purity of heart, urging us not to covet our neighbor's spouse. Joseph's commitment to Mary, and his acceptance of her unique role, show his purity of heart. Living with immense respect and love, without any trace of jealousy or inappropriate desire, Joseph teaches us to cherish pure hearts and intentions, fostering genuine love and respect within our communities.

Finally, the Tenth Commandment, which instructs us not to covet our neighbor's goods, is yet another commandment Saint Joseph lived by instinctively. Though a humble carpenter, he never exhibited greed or envy. His contentment with his life, his work, and his family demonstrates the peace and fulfillment that comes from living within one's means and appreciating what God has provided. This quiet satisfaction contrasts sharply with the unrest born from envy and material desires.

In embodying these commandments, Saint Joseph provides a lived theology that bridges the divine laws and practical life. His existence reflects perfect adherence not as mere duty, but as a committed love for God and neighbor. Each commandment, while presented simply in the Scripture, gains depth and richness when viewed through the prism of Joseph's life.

For Knights of Columbus seeking to consecrate themselves to Saint Joseph, his example offers not only a guide but a road map. By aligning life's actions to the commandments as Joseph did, we find not only compliance with divine law but also profound spiritual fulfillment and a closer communion with God. Saint Joseph's life demonstrates that true observance of the commandments transcends avoidance of wrongdoing; it is about embodying virtues that sanctify everyday life, turning every moment into an act of worship and devotion.

In conclusion, as we strive to live out the Ten Commandments, Saint Joseph stands alongside us as both guide and intercessor. His life, simple yet profound, transforms these divine edicts into attainable paths toward holiness. Such observance, grounded in love and made tangible through Joseph's actions, paves the way for a life of grace, peace, and divine favor.

Aligning Modern Actions with the Commandments

In our ever-evolving world, the challenges we face in aligning our actions with the Commandments are both numerous and complex. The Commandments serve as timeless pillars that guide our moral compass, much like Saint Joseph—whose life was an embodiment of obedience, humility, and righteousness. To truly consecrate ourselves to Saint Joseph, we must examine how our modern actions can align with these eternal laws, creating a seamless harmony between ancient wisdom and contemporary life.

Our first consideration should be the First Commandment: "You shall have no other gods before me." In a society flooded with distractions—be it technology, entertainment, or material achievements—our allegiance to God can easily waver. Here, Saint Joseph's example is particularly instructive. His unwavering faith in God despite manifold uncertainties teaches us to prioritize our spiritual commitments over mundane preoccupations. We must regularly engage in prayer, contemplation, and acts of devotion to maintain our focus on God, eliminating any 'idols' that seek to sidetrack our spiritual journey.

The Second Commandment, "You shall not take the name of the Lord your God in vain," calls us to treat anything sacred—including the use of God's name—with profound respect. Words hold power, and Saint Joseph's silence throughout Scripture speaks volumes. He respected the divine by listening and acting rather than speaking hastily. Emulating his prudent speech in our digital age means we should avoid frivolous or disrespectful mentions of the divine on social media, in casual conversations, and within our inner thoughts. What we say, write, and even think should bring honor to God's name.

Observing the Third Commandment, "Remember the Sabbath day, to keep it holy," appears increasingly challenging in a culture that esteems constant productivity. Saint Joseph, a diligent worker, also knew the importance of rest and worship. By dedicating Sundays to rest and communal worship, we allow ourselves a divine pause to reflect upon our lives and our relationship with God. This practice elevates our existence beyond mere productivity, imbuing it with sacred purpose.

With the Fourth Commandment, "Honor your father and your mother," Saint Joseph provides a poignant lesson in obedience and respect within the family. He honored his familial duties with grace, supporting Mary and Jesus under sometimes daunting circumstances. In today's world, this commandment extends beyond biological ties, encompassing respect for all forms of legitimate authority, as well as extending love and care to the elderly. It is through this lens that we can view our responsibilities as Knights of Columbus, ensuring that we honor and uplift every member of our community.

The Fifth Commandment, "You shall not kill," transcends the mere act of taking life. It encompasses a broader ethic of fostering life—physical, emotional, and spiritual. Saint Joseph's protective nature ensured the safety and well-being of the Holy Family. Modern application calls us to extend this protective care not just to our immediate families but to the broader community, advocating against injustices and supporting life-affirming initiatives everywhere.

Moving to the Sixth Commandment, "You shall not commit adultery," we consider Saint Joseph's chastity and fidelity to Mary. His purity is a model for marital commitments and personal integrity. In a culture often inundated with inappropriate representations of relationships, we are called to purify our hearts, minds, and actions. Upholding the sanctity of marriage and engaging in wholesome, respectful relationships reflects our commitment to this commandment.

The Seventh Commandment, "You shall not steal," compels us to respect others' possessions and rights. Saint Joseph, a modest carpenter, worked honestly to provide for his family, never resorting to dishonest means. Today, this translates into ethical business practices, respect for intellectual property, and a commitment to social justice. Saint Joseph's example reminds us to eschew greed in favor of moral and ethical integrity.

The Eighth Commandment, "You shall not bear false witness against your neighbor," insists on truthfulness and the integrity of our word. Saint Joseph, though silent, spoke volumes through his actions. In a world where misinformation can spread like wildfire, our words must be meticulously chosen to reflect truth and justice. Avoiding gossip and slander, and striving for transparency in our communications fosters a culture of trust grounded in divine truth.

The Ninth Commandment, "You shall not covet your neighbor's wife," and the Tenth Commandment, "You shall not covet your neighbor's goods," guide us in matters of desire and envy. Saint Joseph's life, marked by contentment and dedication, challenges us to find fulfillment in our own circumstances. Modern consumerism often stokes the fires of envy and dissatisfaction. By practicing gratitude and finding joy in our current blessings, we align our desires with God's will, reducing covetous inclinations.

Aligning our actions with all Commandments hinges on our understanding and embodiment of Saint Joseph's virtues. His life furnishes us with a model for modern conduct, turning every activity and thought into an act of consecration. This alignment goes beyond mere compliance—it's about transforming our very being to resonate with divine directives, thus advancing our spiritual journey.

Ultimately, this alignment implores us to cultivate an interior life that mirrors the commandments externally. Each action and decision can then seamlessly reflect our consecration to Saint Joseph. When we view the Commandments not as restrictions but as a pathway to divine harmony, our modern lives become sacred orchestrations, echoing Saint Joseph's faithful adherence to God's will. This transformation not only sanctifies our everyday actions but also leads us ever closer to the heart of God.

Chapter 7: Virtues Exemplified by Saint Joseph

In examining the virtues exemplified by Saint Joseph, we uncover a profound tapestry of humility, obedience, chastity, and patience, each interwoven into the daily fabric of his life. Saint Joseph's humility was not a mere passive resignation but an active engagement, recognizing his role in God's plan without seeking recognition. His unfaltering obedience, as seen in his acceptance of divine instructions, showcased a heart attuned to divine will over personal desire. The virtue of chastity, far from being a negation, embodied a deeper, sacrificial love that mirrored his unique relationship with the Virgin Mary. Patience, a virtue we often undervalue, was illustrated through his steadfast trust during the trials and uncertainties that came with being the earthly guardian of the Holy Family. These virtues, when contemplated and emulated, provide Knights of Columbus a framework for living a life of consecration, aligning one's actions with the higher call of divine service.

The Virtue of Humility

To understand humility, one must first grasp its essence and see how it reflects in the life of Saint Joseph. Humility, in its purest form, is the virtue that enables us to see ourselves as we truly are: beings wholly dependent on God. Saint Joseph, though a man of few words in Scripture, lived this virtue more profoundly than we can fully comprehend. His every action exuded humility, not by self-deprecation, but by his unwavering sense of duty and servitude to the divine will.

Saint Joseph's humility is rooted in his silent obedience to God. He embraced his role as the earthly father of Jesus and the spouse of the Virgin Mary, understanding the immense responsibility it carried. However, he never sought honor for himself. He accepted the tasks entrusted to him without question, embodying humility not just as a passive trait but as an active choice in alignment with God's plan. His humility was not a weakness but a powerful testament to his strength and faith.

Consider the moments of divine instruction that came to Joseph through dreams—the commands to take Mary as his wife, to flee to Egypt, and to return to Israel. Each directive was met with immediate compliance, devoid of hesitation or doubt. Joseph's humility meant trusting in God's wisdom over his own, a difficult feat for any human heart. This trust showcases a profound understanding of his place within the grand narrative of salvation history and underscores the depth of his humility.

In the context of family life, Saint Joseph's humility shone brightly. Despite being the earthly guardian of the Son of God, he took on the role of a simple carpenter. He provided for his family through hard, honest labor, demonstrating that humility is intricately linked with dignity. By working diligently at his trade, he taught Jesus not only about craftsmanship but also about the values of hard work, integrity, and the humility found in serving others.

Saint Joseph's interactions with Mary also reveal his deep humility. When he discovered her pregnancy and considered quietly divorcing her to spare her public disgrace, an angel intervened, revealing the divine plan. Joseph's immediate acceptance and his protective, loving response exemplify his humility. Rather than asserting his rights or demanding explanations, he yielded to God's will, respecting Mary's unique role in salvation history.

In reflecting on Saint Joseph's humility, it is crucial to note that humility is not passivity. Saint Joseph was proactive, a man of action, yet his actions were always aligned with divine guidance. This active humility calls us to evaluate our responses to God's commands and our duties to those around us. Do we accept our roles and responsibilities with the same grace and unwavering trust in God's plan?

Humility in Saint Joseph's life is a pursuit of aligning the self with divine purpose. His every decision, from accepting the angel's messages to undertaking perilous journeys, was driven by humility. This alignment with divine will is an important lesson for us all. It teaches us that true greatness lies not in seeking power or recognition but in allowing God to direct our lives, even when it means embracing obscurity or hardship.

For the Knights of Columbus and all faithful seeking to emulate Saint Joseph, humility is foundational. It demands a readiness to put aside personal ambitions and to serve God's greater glory. In practical terms, this might mean taking on thankless tasks, performing duties without seeking acknowledgment, or supporting others in their missions. It's a call to see the divine in the mundane and the sacred in service.

The humility of Saint Joseph also has a communal dimension. His life teaches us that humility fosters unity. By placing God's will above personal desires, Joseph unified his family through love and service. This unity is especially pertinent for the Knights of Columbus, who are called to brotherhood and collective mission. Embracing humility strengthens this bond and enhances the collective ability to serve the Church and community effectively.

Moreover, humility invites us to a deeper interior life. Saint Joseph's silence in the Gospels is not indicative of a lack of involvement but rather a profound inner life. His silence speaks volumes about his contemplative nature, his ability to reflect deeply on God's mysteries. For theologians and biblical scholars, this aspect of humility is a reminder that true understanding and wisdom often come through quiet reflection and attentive listening to God's whisper in our hearts.

As we strive to embody Saint Joseph's humility, it's beneficial to engage in practices that cultivate this virtue. Daily prayer, reception of the sacraments, meditative reading of Scripture, and sincere acts of charity can help us internalize the humility of Saint Joseph. By dedicating time to these spiritual disciplines, we allow God to shape our hearts and guide our actions, much like He did with Saint Joseph.

Furthermore, humility requires us to acknowledge our limitations and need for God's grace. Saint Joseph's life is a testament to the transformative power of divine grace. His humble acceptance of God's plan and his reliance on divine strength enabled him to fulfill his unique vocation. Similarly, we must recognize that our strength comes from God and that apart from Him, we can do nothing. This recognition is not a cause for despair but a source of hope, for it is in our weakness that God's power is made perfect.

In conclusion, the virtue of humility as exemplified by Saint Joseph is a call to trust, serve, reflect, and unite. His life provides us with a roadmap for how to live humbly in our modern context, serving God and others with love and dedication. As Knights of Columbus, theologians, and faithful Catholics, may we draw inspiration from Saint Joseph's humility and strive to incorporate this virtue into our lives, allowing it to transform our hearts and actions in the service of God and His Church.

The Virtue of Obedience

In the annals of salvation history, Saint Joseph stands as a paragon of obedience. His life, a quiet symphony of compliance to the Divine Will, offers us profound lessons on the virtue of obedience. For the members of the Knights of Columbus, understanding and emulating this virtue is essential to living a consecrated life devoted to Saint Joseph.

Saint Joseph's obedience is first and foremost illustrated in his response to God's messages conveyed through the angel. "Joseph, son of David, do not be afraid to take Mary as your wife," the angel instructed in a dream (Matthew 1:20). Joseph promptly obeyed, notwithstanding the potential social stigma and personal uncertainty. His immediate compliance signifies a heart attuned to the divine directives, prioritizing God's plan over his own.

But what's particularly noteworthy about Joseph's obedience is its quiet, unassuming nature. Unlike many figures in scripture, Joseph's actions speak louder than words. He doesn't debate or question God; he listens and acts. This silent obedience speaks volumes about his humility and trust in God's wisdom.

It is worth reflecting on how obedience shaped the practical aspects of Joseph's life. As a carpenter, he would have had his own plans and schedules. Yet, when instructed to flee to Egypt with Mary and Jesus to escape Herod's wrath, he did so without hesitation (Matthew 2:13-14). This readiness to inconvenience himself, to upend his life and move to a foreign land, underscores that true obedience often requires sacrifice. It challenges us to consider: how willing are we to obey God when it disrupts our plans?

Equally important is the obedience Saint Joseph showed toward civil and religious laws. He took Mary to Bethlehem for the census, obeying the decree of Caesar Augustus (Luke 2:1-5). He presented Jesus in the temple and observed all the rituals stipulated by the law (Luke 2:22-24). Joseph's adherence to both divine and human laws reflects a comprehensive obedience that encompasses all aspects of life.

Saint Joseph's obedience also embodies a profound trust in the providence of God. Trust and obedience are two sides of the same coin. You can't have one without the other. Joseph's trust is evident during the flight to Egypt and their subsequent return to Nazareth when the angel again instructs him (Matthew 2:19-23). Through these transitions, Joseph relied not on his understanding but on the directions given by God. For the Knights of Columbus, this trust is a crucial element. Obeying God's will, even when the path is unclear, requires a firm belief in His omniscience and benevolence.

The allegorical significance of Joseph's obedience goes even deeper. Obedience, in Joseph's life, is not mere compliance. It is a testament to his unwavering love and respect for God. This love-driven obedience is akin to the knight's loyalty to his liege—a devotion that transcends duty and enters the realm of sincere fidelity.

We, too, are called to manifest such love-driven obedience in our daily lives. It's an obedience that goes beyond mere rule-following. It requires a heart transformed by grace, one that willingly seeks to align with God's will. C.S. Lewis once opined that "obedience is the road to freedom." To truly grasp this, we need to understand that obedience to God liberates us from our selfish desires, allowing us to partake in the divine plan.

In the realm of the Knights of Columbus, this obedience translates into service—service to the Church, to our communities, and to our families. Just as Joseph served Mary and Jesus, we are called to serve those entrusted to our care. This service, stemming from obedience, becomes an avenue for living out our consecration to Saint Joseph.

Furthermore, the allegory of Joseph's obedience can be seen in our contemporary duties and responsibilities. In our world, where autonomy and personal freedom are often exalted, Joseph teaches us that true greatness lies in the submission to divine authority. He didn't seek his own glory. Instead, he found glory in serving God's purposes, fulfilling his role in a divine narrative written long before time began.

Saint Paul writes in Philippians 2:8, "He humbled himself by becoming obedient to death—even death on a cross." While this refers to Christ's ultimate act of obedience, Joseph's life foreshadows this sacrifice. By obeying God's immediate directives, Joseph sets the stage for Christ's ultimate act of obedience. Thus, in a very real sense, Joseph's obedience is part of the salvific arc that culminates in Christ's Passion and Resurrection.

In cultivating the virtue of obedience, we must be prepared to embrace both the mundane and the miraculous. Joseph didn't only obey in monumental moments; his life was a continuum of obedience in the ordinary. From his daily work as a carpenter to the more significant moments of divine intervention, Joseph's life was a testament to consistent, unwavering obedience.

In a culture that often lauds rebellion and self-determination, Joseph's example of obedience offers a counter-narrative. It's a narrative that speaks of humility, trust, and unwavering faith. For the

Knights of Columbus, this counter-cultural stance is pivotal. It roots us in a tradition that values God's wisdom over human understanding, prioritizes divine directives over personal ambition, and esteems sacrificial service over self-aggrandizement.

Therefore, as members of the Knights of Columbus, let us strive to cultivate the virtue of obedience in our lives. Let us look to Saint Joseph as our exemplar, embodying the principles he so quietly yet profoundly demonstrated. Let our obedience be not just an outward adherence but an inward transformation that aligns our hearts with God's will.

This transformative obedience is, in essence, an act of love. Just as Joseph's love for God and his family propelled his obedience, so should our love for God, our families, and our communities compel us to live obediently. In doing so, we honor not only Saint Joseph but also the God he so faithfully served.

In conclusion, the virtue of obedience, as exemplified by Saint Joseph, is a cornerstone for living a life of consecration. It calls for a radical trust, a humble submission, and a heartfelt devotion to God's will. May Saint Joseph, the obedient servant, guide and inspire us on this path, leading us closer to the heart of God.

The Virtue of Chastity

Chastity, as exemplified by Saint Joseph, is a profound virtue, deeply rooted in his unwavering love and respect for the Virgin Mary, as well as his total consecration to God. To understand the virtue of chastity in the life of Saint Joseph, we must start by reflecting on the sacred and unbroken union between him and Mary. Theirs was a marriage of unparalleled purity, a union ordained by God himself to shelter the most holy human family in history.

In the context of their marriage, Joseph's chastity wasn't simply a matter of abstinence; it was a higher calling to purity and self-sacrifice. He embraced his role as the guardian of Mary's virginity with steadfast commitment, recognizing that his task was to protect and honor God's divine plan. This understanding transforms chastity from a mere personal discipline into a profound act of love and devotion.

In a world often plagued by disordered desires and temptations, Saint Joseph stands as a beacon of purity. His life challenges us to view chastity not as a limitation but as a liberation. Through chastity, one is freed to love purely and wholly, unencumbered by selfish desires. Joseph's chaste heart allowed him to love Mary with a purity that reflects divine love, teaching us that chastity is intrinsically linked to true, selfless love.

Moreover, Saint Joseph's chastity was intertwined with his humility and obedience. He accepted the divine mystery entrusted to him without seeking personal gratification. This virtue was aligned with his overarching mission to serve and protect. His humility fortified his commitment to chastity, reminding us that surrendering to God's will often requires renunciation of personal desires and the cultivation of inner purity.

Analogously, the Fathers of the Church have long held that chastity is a form of spiritual warriorhood. Saint Joseph, as a spiritual warrior, guarded the sanctity of his family with his purity. His chaste heart was his shield, his unyielding faith his weapon. In this light, chastity becomes a powerful testament to one's inner strength and dedication to God's will.

Saint Joseph's life also offers practical guidance for Knights of Columbus who aspire to live out this virtue. Modern society presents numerous challenges to living a life of chastity. To follow Joseph's example requires vigilance and steadfastness. Knights can turn to Saint Joseph for strength, remembering that chastity is not just about abstinence but about respecting the sacredness of their bodies and those of others.

Engaging in daily prayer and seeking the intercession of Saint Joseph can fortify one's resolve to live chastely. The act of consecration to Saint Joseph serves as a daily renewal of this commitment, aligning one's will with God's and seeking divine assistance in the pursuit of purity. Through consistent prayer, Knights can develop a deeper relationship with Saint Joseph, drawing from his strength and purity.

Chastity also has a communal aspect. It contributes to the well-being of the family and the wider community. By upholding this virtue, Knights can foster stronger, more authentic relationships, built on mutual respect and love. Saint Joseph's life exemplifies that chastity is integral to the health and sanctity of the Christian family.

Also, chastity, when viewed through the lens of Saint Joseph's actions, goes beyond personal morality; it becomes a reflection of one's dedication to God and His divine plan. The purity of heart and intention that Joseph personified is a call to all to purify their own lives, making them a fitting vessel for God's work.

It's significant to note that chastity for Saint Joseph was an active choice, embraced with firm intention every day. It was not merely an avoidance of sin but a proactive pursuit of virtue. Knights of Columbus can take inspiration from his example by mindfully choosing purity and seeking support within their community to maintain their commitment.

Saint Joseph also teaches that chastity involves a measured balance of love and self-control. His ability to love Mary and Jesus in such a pure, untarnished way is a testament to the power of controlled and disciplined affections. Modern Knights can aspire to this level of purity in their relationships, allowing love to flourish without the shadows of selfish desires.

In conclusion, the virtue of chastity as exemplified by Saint Joseph serves as an essential pillar for Knights of Columbus who are dedicated to consecration. His life encourages us to look beyond the mere abstinence, to a higher calling of purity and selfless love. By embracing chastity, Knights not only honor God's will but also bring about a transformation in their personal lives, their families, and their communities, fostering a culture of respect, love, and divine commitment.

The Virtue of Patience

Patience is a virtue lauded extensively in Scripture and exemplified profoundly by Saint Joseph. In a world that often celebrates immediacy and instant gratification, understanding the depth of Saint Joseph's patience provides us with a countercultural paradigm that is both instructional and deeply theological. The life of Saint Joseph, though often shrouded in the background of Jesus and Mary, unfolds a story rich with quiet endurance and steadfast trust in God's timing.

Saint Joseph's patience is not a passive waiting but an active, engaged anticipation. Consider the annunciation of Mary's unique circumstances. When he first learned of Mary's pregnancy, Joseph faced a profound personal dilemma. According to Mosaic law, he had the right to expose Mary to public disgrace or even worse. Yet, he chose a path of compassionate withdrawal, deciding to divorce her quietly. This decision, however, was halted by the intervention of an angel, which further highlighted Joseph's capacity for patience. He didn't react hastily but waited for divine guidance, showing a balance of justice and mercy.

Joseph's life demonstrates that patience is often intertwined with humility and obedience. His waiting is a fruit of his unwavering faith and trust in God, which are virtues deeply resonant in the spiritual journey. This form of patience is not born out of reluctance but out of a conscious choice to trust in divine providence. Imagine the patience required to raise the Son of God. The daily, sometimes mundane, but profoundly significant tasks of fatherhood were for Joseph opportunities to exercise this virtue. Each moment carried the weight of divine purpose, yet he fulfilled his role without clamoring for recognition or reward.

One can also view Joseph's journey to Bethlehem and the subsequent flight to Egypt as stages in his spiritual maturation, shaped by patience. The arduous travels, marked by uncertainty and danger, required immense perseverance. Joseph did not question or resist; instead, he remained patient and devoted to his family's safety and God's will. These acts weren't grandiose; they didn't involve miracles or supernatural signs but were simple, profound manifestations of divine patience.

Theological reflections place patience at the heart of Christian discipleship. It's through patience that one learns to align personal will with divine will. Observing Saint Joseph's life invites us to contemplate our own responses to trials and uncertainties. In a spiritual context, patience involves trusting in God's timing and understanding that delays and detours can serve a greater purpose. Joseph's acceptance of God's plan, without intermediary cessation, provides a template for our own acceptances in the journey of faith.

Philosophically, patience can be seen as a form of self-mastery. It's the ability to wait calmly in the face of frustration or adversity. Saint Joseph embodies this ideal. He mastered his desires and inclinations, choosing instead the path of disciplined self-control. This wasn't a suppression of action but a channeling of energy into constructive and purposeful fulfillment of duties. The quiet strength of patience, as seen in Saint Joseph, contrasts sharply with the often chaotic, impulsive reactions of the modern world.

In our daily life, patience allows us to confront challenges with a composed and resilient spirit. By emulating Saint Joseph, we learn to manage our expectations and maintain our focus on long-term goals rather than short-term satisfactions. His life teaches us that patience involves an inherent hope—an anticipation grounded not in idle waiting but in active engagement with God's unfolding plan.

For the Knights of Columbus, consecrating one's life to Saint Joseph involves adopting his virtues, patience chief among them. The order's commitment to charitable works, spiritual development, and communal support mirrors the patient dedication Joseph displayed. In every act of service, whether grand or humble, patience ensures that the Knight remains steadfast in purpose and compassionate in action.

Furthermore, patience shapes our spiritual and communal identity. It fosters harmony and understanding, essential in any community devoted to shared values and goals. By looking to Saint Joseph, members of the Knights of Columbus can cultivate a deeper sense of unity and cohesiveness, grounded in the mutual respect and enduring commitment that patience affords.

Patience also deepens our prayer life. It encourages a rhythm of stillness and listening, allowing us to discern God's voice amid the noise of our daily existence. Saint Joseph's example teaches us that prayer is not always about speaking but often about waiting and listening. This contemplative patience nurtures a deeper, more intimate relationship with God, allowing for a transformative spiritual growth that aligns us closer with His divine will.

In conclusion, the virtue of patience, as exemplified by Saint Joseph, is a cornerstone for those aspiring to consecrate themselves to his patronage. It challenges the quick fixes and immediate results that dominate contemporary culture, urging instead a return to trust and deliberate action. For the Knights of Columbus, this patience shapes not only personal spirituality but also communal efforts, ensuring every endeavor is rooted in thoughtful compassion and resilient faith. Following Joseph's patient path, we find a roadmap for a life attuned to divine will and the higher calling of service, faith, and unwavering trust in God's perfect timing.

Chapter 8: Principles of Natural Law

To delve into the principles of natural law is to explore the unwritten code that governs all of creation, a sublime and immutable order reflecting the divine wisdom of the Creator. Saint Joseph, in his earthly life, serves as a perfect exemplar of adherence to natural law, embodying the virtues that align humanity with God's eternal design. This law, rooted in reason and accessible to human intellect, offers an intrinsic guide to morality and righteousness, calling us to discern and actualize the good in our every action. It is neither a mere philosophical construct nor a rigid legalistic framework, but rather a living testament to God's will etched in the fabric of our existence. Through the lens of Catholic understanding, we recognize that the principles of natural law are intrinsic to our nature, urging us towards justice, truth, and love. Saint Joseph's silent yet powerful witness aids us in perceiving these principles not as abstract ideals, but as concrete paths to holiness and divine union. As Knights of Columbus, our consecration to Saint Joseph invites us to embody these principles, navigating the complexities of modern life with a steadfast commitment to divine truth and moral integrity. The virtuous life, shaped by the natural law, becomes not only a personal journey of sanctification but also a beacon of Christ's light to a world in dire need of ethical clarity and moral courage.

Defining Natural Law in Catholicism

The concept of natural law in Catholicism is both ancient and deeply rooted in theological tradition. It stands as a beacon of moral clarity, arising from the understanding that God has imprinted certain innate principles upon the human heart. These principles guide human behavior toward the ultimate good and align it with divine reason. As knights consecrated to Saint Joseph, you are called to not merely understand but to manifest these principles in your daily lives.

Natural law, in its essence, is the participation of human beings in God's eternal law through reason and free will. It is a law 'written in the hearts' of men, as the Apostle Paul mentions in his letter to the Romans (Romans 2:15). This instilled law directs us toward actions that fulfill our true purpose: to love God and love our neighbor. It serves as an inner compass, pointing us toward virtuous living and away from actions that harm our relationship with the Creator and His creation.

At its core, natural law is universal. It transcends cultural and temporal boundaries, binding all people regardless of time or place. This universality underscores the objective nature of moral truths. In the words of Saint Thomas Aquinas, natural law is "nothing else than the rational creature's participation in the eternal law." Here, Aquinas emphasizes that through the exercise of human reason, we discern the fundamental precepts of this law: to do good and avoid evil.

In the context of Catholicism, natural law is not a mere philosophical abstraction but a lived reality. It engages the believer in a continuous process of moral discernment and action. Consequently, understanding natural law helps the consecrated knight to appreciate the inherent dignity of human life, the sanctity of marriage and family, and the imperative of both justice and charity in social relations.

The life of Saint Joseph offers a poignant illustration of natural law in action. His ceaseless adherence to God's will, his unwavering commitment to the Holy Family, and his integrity in labor exemplify natural law's principles. The silent witness of Joseph's life articulates the harmony between reason and divine command. He provides a model for living in accord with God's law, revealing how human virtue can mirror divine goodness.

Natural law speaks to the order and purpose woven into the fabric of creation. It suggests that there are truths about human nature and destiny that can be known through reason, even apart from divine revelation. Yet, in Catholic thought, these natural truths find their fullest expression and deepest fulfillment in the light of faith. Revelation does not contradict natural law but rather, elevates and perfects it. Faith illuminates those corners of moral knowledge that reason alone might only partially grasp.

As knights devoted to Saint Joseph, your lives must reflect these principles through discernment and action. The very act of consecration invites you to a deeper understanding of natural law, urging you to become stewards of God's created order. This duty encompasses every aspect of life, from personal conduct to public engagement, always reflecting the inherent truths of natural law.

Consider the implications of natural law on issues of justice and human rights. Every human being, fashioned in the image of God, possesses inherent dignity and worth. This belief compels us to defend life, oppose injustice, and work toward the common good. As followers of Saint Joseph, your mission includes advocating for the vulnerable, protecting the sanctity of life, and upholding the principles of social justice rooted in natural law.

Furthermore, natural law provides a framework for evaluating moral choices and societal laws. It insists that civil laws must align with the moral order inscribed by God in human nature. When human laws deviate from this order, they lose their binding moral force. This perspective has significant implications for your vocation, whether confronting ethical dilemmas in professional life or navigating complex social issues.

In your consecration to Saint Joseph, a deepened understanding of natural law enriches your moral and spiritual life. It enables you to cultivate virtues, not as abstract ideals but as concrete expressions of God's will. Humility, obedience, chastity, patience—all these virtues exemplified by Saint Joseph—are fruits of living in harmony with natural law. They mold your character and direct your actions toward true goodness.

The pedagogical aspect of natural law also deserves attention. As leaders within your communities, you have a responsibility to educate others about these enduring moral truths. This education extends beyond mere instruction; it involves guiding others in the practical application of natural law. Through your example and mentorship, you help others understand how to live justly, love fully, and serve God's purposes faithfully.

Natural law thus stands as a cornerstone of Catholic moral teaching. It bridges the gap between faith and reason, revelation and human nature. By deeply engaging with this teaching, you honor Saint Joseph's legacy and fortify your commitment to living as consecrated knights, defenders of God's truth, and exemplars of His love.

Living Out Natural Law Principles

In the context of natural law, the principles are eternal, unchanging truths that guide human actions toward good and away from evil. Living out these principles isn't merely a matter of ethical consideration but a deeply spiritual endeavor rooted in aligning one's life with the divine order established by God. For the Roman Catholic, particularly Knights of Columbus striving for consecration to Saint Joseph, embracing these principles is a pathway to holiness.

Saint Joseph himself serves as an exemplar of living out natural law. His life exemplified adherence to the natural moral order through his roles as a father, husband, and worker. His actions were always in harmony with God's will, a manifestation of prudence, justice, fortitude, and temperance—the cardinal virtues that are cornerstones of natural law.

Consider natural law's principle of pursuing good and avoiding evil. In Joseph's decision to take Mary as his wife despite the societal shame attached to her pregnancy, we witness his deep moral conviction and justice. He sought not his own comfort but adhered to a higher moral good, exemplifying the right use of the intellect and will oriented toward the divine plan.

Similarly, his work as a carpenter underlines the principle of contributing to the common good. Work, under natural law, is more than a means to an end; it's a vocation through which individuals participate in God's creation. Joseph's diligent labor provided for the Holy Family, sanctifying the ordinary act of work and demonstrating its intrinsic value in human life.

Naturally, families form the backbone of society, per natural law. Joseph's devoted fatherhood offers a model of paternal duty, aligning with the principle that the family is the primary cell of social life. By nurturing Jesus and providing for Mary, Joseph honored the natural law's emphasis on familial bonds and responsibilities, further underlining the sacredness of the familial sphere.

On a societal level, living out natural law involves creating and supporting structures that reflect moral order. Knights of Columbus, drawing from Joseph's example, are called to build and sustain communities that promote common good, subsidiarity, and solidarity. These principles drive the Knights to engage in charitable works, advocacy for life, and support for the vulnerable, thereby infusing society with the values inherent in natural law.

Consider the principle of the sanctity of human life, intrinsic to natural law. Joseph's protection of Mary and Jesus highlights his unwavering commitment to life's sacredness. In today's context, Knights can champion causes that uphold the dignity of life at all stages, from conception to natural death, rallying against issues that threaten this fundamental principle.

Justice, another pillar of natural law, can be seen in Joseph's fair treatment of all he encountered. He recognized the inherent worth in every person, reflecting the divine image in humanity. This aspect of natural law calls Knights of Columbus to act justly in their interactions, ensuring fairness and advocating for those unjustly treated, reflecting the divine justice embodied by Joseph.

Prudence is the practical wisdom that allows us to discern true good in every circumstance and choose the right means of achieving it. Saint Joseph's thoughtful and discerning nature made him the prudent guardian of the Holy Family. Knights, in their decision-making processes—whether personal, professional, or communal—can look to Joseph's prudence as a guide, ensuring their choices reflect true good and divine will.

Temperance, the moderating influence on desires, ensuring they remain within reasonable bounds, was evident in Joseph's life of simplicity and fidelity. By practicing temperance, Knights emulate his example, balancing their lives, avoiding excesses, and focusing on what genuinely nurtures their spiritual and communal well-being.

Thus, living out natural law principles isn't a passive undertaking but a dynamic process of constant alignment with God's eternal truths. It involves an active commitment to virtues, embodied in the life and actions of Saint Joseph, offering a constant guide for Knights of Columbus.

In sum, the integration of natural law into everyday life draws us into a deeper communion with God's divine order. It requires mindfulness and dedication, enabling actions to resonate harmoniously with the moral compass given to humanity by the Creator. Through Saint Joseph, Catholics, especially Knights of Columbus, find a tangible blueprint for this high calling, blending moral principles with vibrant, lived faith, ensuring their journey towards consecration is both meaningful and rooted in divine wisdom.

Chapter 9: Original Consecration Prayers

In those sacred moments when words ascend to the heavens, the act of consecration to Saint Joseph becomes more than a ritual—it transforms into a profound dialogue between the soul and the celestial guardian. The "Prayer of Consecration to Saint Joseph" channels our deepest yearnings for guidance, invoking his unparalleled virtues of humility, obedience, and strength. By engaging in "Daily Devotions to Saint Joseph," one integrates these momentous supplications into the rhythm of daily life, allowing the spirit to be constantly nurtured under his protection. The "Knight's Prayer for Divine Assistance" further sanctifies the journey of Knights of Columbus, fortifying their resolve with divine grace. Thus, these original prayers are not mere utterances but sacred oaths, binding us intimately with Saint Joseph's divine patronage.

Prayer of Consecration to Saint Joseph

In the sacred bounds of Catholic tradition, consecration stands as a profound act of devotion, a commitment of one's entire being to divine service. The "Prayer of Consecration to Saint Joseph" encapsulates this commitment, focusing particularly on Saint Joseph's unique role in salvation history. Integrating theological depth with devotional fervor, this prayer serves as both an individual and communal dedication.

Saint Joseph, the quiet but stalwart figure of the Gospels, has often been overlooked in the shadow of more prominent biblical characters. However, his life exemplifies a relentless adherence to God's will, making him a beacon for those on the path of consecration. It is within this context that we approach the "Prayer of Consecration to Saint Joseph," seeking his intercession and model of virtue.

Before delving into the actual prayer, it is critical to understand its theological anchor. Consecration in the Catholic sense involves setting oneself apart for God, sanctifying oneself through a vow, and by extension, integrating Saint Joseph's virtues into one's daily life. Known for his humility, obedience, and unwavering faith, Saint Joseph provides a template for living a life consecrated to divine service.

In invoking Saint Joseph through consecration, we not only seek his intercession but also ask to embody his virtues. Humility stands at the forefront. Saint Joseph's humility was displayed in his acceptance of God's plan, despite the uncertainties and potential for public scorn. His obedience to divine messages, conveyed through dreams, reflects a steadfast trust in God's providence.

The "Prayer of Consecration to Saint Joseph" invites devotees to align their lives more closely with these virtues. Each recitation deepens the bonds between the faithful and Saint Joseph, fostering an environment where God's will can be discerned and followed more clearly. It is an act that calls for introspection, a reevaluation of one's priorities, and a genuine commitment to spiritual growth.

One might ask, what specific elements should be present in such a consecration prayer? The prayer should begin with an invocation, calling upon Saint Joseph to hear our prayers and intercede on our behalf. This is followed by an acknowledgment of his virtues—his purity, diligence, and fatherly care. The heart of the prayer should then express a personal commitment to embody these virtues, and a plea for the courage and strength to live a life in harmony with God's will.

Let us proceed with a structured form of the "Prayer of Consecration to Saint Joseph." Each line is carefully crafted to reflect the depth of our devotion and the sincerity of our commitment.

1. Invocation: O Glorious Saint Joseph, foster-father of Jesus and spouse of the Blessed Virgin Mary, we place ourselves under your most holy protection.
2. Acknowledgment of Virtues: With reverence, we acknowledge your virtues: your unwavering faith, steadfast humility, diligent labor, and most chaste heart.

3. Commitment: Inspired by your example, we consecrate ourselves wholly to your paternal care. We pledge to emulate your virtues, living a life of humility, obedience, and holiness.
4. Plea for Intercession: Dear Saint Joseph, protect us from sin, guide us in our work, and lead us on the path of righteousness. May our families reflect the holy family, and our actions bring glory to God.

In engaging with this prayer daily, we not only invite Saint Joseph's intercession but also cultivate a habit of reflection and alignment with divine will. This routine, over time, transforms our spiritual landscape, allowing a deeper and more profound relationship with God.

Moreover, this consecration is not a solitary act but a communal one. When families, parish groups, or Knights of Columbus councils come together to pray, they strengthen the communal ties that bind them to Saint Joseph and, by extension, to one another. This collective act of devotion imbues the community with strength, resilience, and a shared sense of purpose rooted in the divine.

It is crucial to remember that, while the words of the prayer are vital, the disposition of the heart is equally important. Consecration to Saint Joseph requires more than mere recitation; it demands a genuine openness to transformation. By consistently revisiting the values encapsulated in this prayer, we nurture a spirit of ongoing conversion.

In conclusion, the "Prayer of Consecration to Saint Joseph" serves as a spiritual roadmap, guiding the faithful towards a more profound union with God through the intercession and example of Saint Joseph. It is both a personal and communal act that, when embraced fully, can lead to substantial spiritual growth. As we consecrate ourselves, let us do so with a heart open to the transformative power of God's grace, ever mindful of Saint Joseph's humble and obedient example.

Daily Devotions to Saint Joseph

In the pursuit of deeper consecration to Saint Joseph, daily devotions play an integral role. Each day can be imbued with moments that cultivate an intimate relationship with Saint Joseph, fostering a life rich in spiritual growth and sanctity. The following daily devotions offer both structure and freedom, encouraging a rhythm of prayer that aligns with one's personal journey and commitments.

Begin each morning with a simple, yet profound prayer to Saint Joseph. As the day unfolds, this initial invocation sets the tone for a day lived under his guidance and protection. Such a prayer can be as brief as, "Saint Joseph, patron of the Universal Church, protect me today as you protected Jesus and Mary. Guide my thoughts, words, and actions."

Incorporate an examination of your conscience in the morning or evening, reflecting upon your actions through the lens of Saint Joseph's virtues. His humility, obedience, and patience serve as benchmarks for personal reflection. Ask yourself: "In what ways have I emulated Saint Joseph today? In what areas can I improve?" This practice not only fosters personal growth but also deepens your alignment with the virtues emblematic of Saint Joseph.

Reciting the Litany of Saint Joseph is another daily devotion that enriches the soul. The litany, with its series of invocations, serves as a powerful reminder of the multifaceted roles Saint Joseph plays in the lives of the faithful. Each title—such as "Joseph most prudent" and "Terror of demons"—is a meditation in itself, inviting you to contemplate different aspects of his sanctity and seek his intercession in specific areas of your life.

An especially poignant moment in daily devotions is the mid-day prayer. The Angelus at noon, traditionally dedicated to the Annunciation, can be adapted to include a prayer to Saint Joseph. This interlude of prayer amidst daily activities serves as a powerful reminder of Saint Joseph's constant presence and support. "Saint Joseph, guardian of the Holy Family, be with me in my daily tasks," might be a fitting addition to your usual prayers.

Reading scripture that highlights the life and actions of Saint Joseph is another valuable practice. While Saint Joseph does not speak in the Gospels, his actions are profound and instructive. Meditate on passages such as Matthew 1:18-25 and Luke 2:41-52. Reflect on his silent obedience, his protective nature, and his unwavering faith. Allow these reflections to inform your daily actions, striving to mirror his fidelity and trust in God.

In the evening, devote time to a rosary with a special focus on the Joyful Mysteries. Each mystery reflects moments intimately connected to Saint Joseph's life and mission. Pondering these mysteries can deepen your understanding of his role in salvation history and inspire you to emulate his virtues. For instance, meditate on the Nativity and consider Saint Joseph's quiet strength in the face of uncertainty. How can you bring that same strength to your own life challenges?

Additionally, integrate a nightly prayer thanking Saint Joseph for his protection and guidance throughout the day. This prayer might simply be, "Thank you, Saint Joseph, for watching over me and guiding my steps today. Help me to sleep peacefully and to rise tomorrow with a renewed commitment to follow your example." Such a prayer fosters a sense of gratitude and reliance on Saint Joseph's intercession, promoting peace and restfulness.

Adoring Saint Joseph through acts of charity is another practical way of living out your consecration. Alms-giving, visiting the sick, and supporting those in need are all ways of honoring Saint Joseph's legacy. His life was marked by selfless service, and by mirroring this, you draw closer to his spirit. Each act of kindness becomes a devotion in itself, reflecting the love and care that Saint Joseph showed to Jesus and Mary.

The inclusion of Saint Joseph in the family's daily routine can also be significant. Establishing a small home altar dedicated to him, adorned with his image and perhaps a candle, serves as a visual and physical reminder of his presence. Family prayers said at this altar can infuse the household with a sense of sacredness and communal spirit, strengthened by Saint Joseph's example of family dedication.

Monthly, consider dedicating a first Wednesday devotion to Saint Joseph, reflecting the Church's custom. Attend Mass if possible, offering the Eucharist in his honor, and engage in extended prayer or a spiritual retreat. These monthly devotions allow for a deeper, periodic reflection on your consecration journey, recalibrating your heart and mind towards Saint Joseph's virtues.

Learning from the saints who had a particular devotion to Saint Joseph can also fortify your own daily practices. Saints such as Teresa of Avila, who found in him a powerful intercessor and protector, provide insights and examples that can be emulated in your devotions. By reading their works and prayers dedicated to Saint Joseph, you enrich your own spiritual practice with the wisdom of their experiences.

Finally, private vows or commitments made to live out specific virtues in honor of Saint Joseph can be beneficial. These could include commitments to purity, humility, or fidelity, reflecting the aspects of Saint Joseph's life that are most meaningful to you. By making and adhering to these personal vows, your daily actions become continuous acts of devotion to Saint Joseph, aligning your life more closely with his holy example.

Daily devotions to Saint Joseph are not merely routines but avenues through which the Holy Spirit can work within you, molding your heart to mirror Saint Joseph's. While each devotion is an expression of love and reverence, collectively they create a tapestry of faith that envelops your day, sanctifying even the most mundane tasks. Through these devotions, you not only draw closer to Saint Joseph but also deepen your relationship with Jesus and Mary, fostering a holistic approach to your spiritual life.

As you incorporate these practices into your daily routine, remember the profound impact that a life consecrated to Saint Joseph can have. In his quiet strength, humble service, and unwavering commitment to God's will, Saint Joseph stands as a beacon of virtue and faith. Let your daily devotions be a testament to your dedication, allowing his example to illuminate your path and transform your life. By consistently turning to Saint Joseph, you align yourself with a legacy of holiness and draw ever closer to the heart of God.

Knight's Prayer for Divine Assistance

O Saint Joseph, our mighty patron, we turn to you who faithfully guarded and guided the Holy Family with unwavering dedication. As Knights of Columbus, we stand together in this moment, seeking your divine assistance to gird our spirits and direct our endeavors. Just as you were called upon to protect Jesus and Mary, we are summoned to protect our communities, our families, and our faith.

Saint Joseph, who rises as a luminary of patience and courage, endow us with the fortitude to withstand the challenges we encounter daily. Our hearts are laden with both the moral and temporal crises of our times, and we ask that your unwavering trust in God shine as a beacon in our darkest hours. Make our faith as solid as the carpenter's wood you once held in your own blessed hands.

Almighty intercessor, we call upon your strength to guide us in our roles as protectors of the Church and its teachings. Enable us to be resilient and firm, not in our own power, but through grace bestowed upon us by following your exemplary path. You, who were divinely chosen to guard the Redeemer, teach us the essence of guardianship in our modern world. May we emulate your vigilance and provide a sanctuary of faith for those entrusted to our care.

Through your diligent labor in the humble town of Nazareth, you manifested the dignity of work infused with love and devotion. Enlighten us to see beyond the mundane in our everyday tasks, revealing the sacred nature of our labor when performed in service to God's greater glory. Let us, too, find joy and purpose in our vocations, turning even the simplest acts into offerings of reverence and praise.

In your chastity and purity, you remained a devoted spouse to Mary, the Mother of God. Teach us the sanctity of marital relations, binding us in mutual respect and divine love. As Knights, many of us are fathers and husbands, aspiring to mirror the holy model you set. Impart to us the wisdom to honor and cherish our families, leading them closer to Christ through both word and example.

Saint Joseph, you who are the epitome of fatherhood, we ask for your guidance in the spiritual upbringing of our children. May we never falter in our duty to instill in them the values of our faith. Just as you nurtured Jesus, the Son of God, help us to nurture our children in the light of His teachings. Foster within us a spirit of tenderness mixed with discipline, ensuring that the young ones under our guardianship grow into strong pillars of faith.

Lover of poverty, who chose a life of simplicity and detachment from worldly allurements, inspire us to seek spiritual riches over material gain. Guide us to use our resources wisely, not for personal aggrandizement, but for the upliftment of the less fortunate. Teach us the true meaning of charity and compel us to live out the beatitudes in every aspect of our lives. In doing so, we aim to create a thriving, just society modeled after the kingdom of Heaven.

Just as you heeded the angel's message without hesitation, let our hearts be open to God's will, even when it demands sacrifices of us. Illuminate our path with obedient surrender, adapting our desires to align with the Divine Will. Strengthen our resolve to act promptly and faithfully, regardless of the uncertainties that lie before us.

O Saint Joseph, who was named the Terror of Demons, fortify us in our spiritual battles against evil. Clad us in the armor of righteousness, imbue us with the skill to wield the sword of prayer. As Knights, we are engaged in perpetual combat against the principalities and powers of darkness. Shield us from every snare of the enemy, and by your intercession, keep us steadfast in our pursuit of holiness.

Your demise was serene, flanked by the love of Jesus and Mary. Prepare us for a similar end, steeped in peace and bolstered by the sacraments. Let our deaths be as our lives—rooted firmly in God's love. Pray that we may enter into eternal glory, united with you in the heavenly realms, forever praising the Divine Majesty.

Oh Chaste Spouse of the Blessed Virgin, you who are most valiant, hear the supplications of your devoted Knights. For we know that in invoking your name and seeking your counsel, we are led closer to the Sacred Heart of Jesus. Assist us in every undertaking, making each a testament to the faith and commitment that so gloriously adorned your life.

Saint Joseph, foster father of our Savior and defender of sinners, bestow upon us the spiritual armor needed to fulfill our divine missions. We implore your benevolence, knowing well that your benevolence is boundless. With your aid, let us pave a path of righteousness that others may follow, thereby manifesting Christ's presence in a world yearning for His grace.

We close this prayer with hearts full of hope and souls aflame with purpose. We submit humbly to God's sweetest providence, trusting in your guidance and unwavering support. Grant that, through your continual intercession, we may serve as true Knights of Columbus, ever valiant in our devotion, eager in our labor, loving in our leadership, and firm in our faith.

Amen.

Chapter 10: Practical Applications

In our journey of consecration to Saint Joseph, it is vital to integrate our spiritual commitments with the realities of daily life. Fostering a devotional life involves setting aside regular time for prayer and reflection, allowing the sanctity and wisdom of Saint Joseph to permeate our routines. Balancing secular duties with religious commitments means imitating Saint Joseph's dedication as a worker and a guardian while fulfilling our vocations in the world. Community engagement through faith challenges us to extend our devotion beyond personal practice, encouraging us to bring the light of Saint Joseph into our interactions with others. By these applications, we can transform ordinary actions into extraordinary acts of faith, embodying the virtues and strength of Saint Joseph in our roles as Knights of Columbus.

Fostering a Devotional Life

Fostering a devotional life, especially one centered around Saint Joseph, demands a combination of intention, education, and habitual practices. Such a life isn't cultivated overnight; it requires continual nurturing and mindfulness. In the fast-paced modern world, commitment to a devoted life roots itself in the stability of tradition, the serenity of daily rituals, and the transformative power of prayer. The Knights of Columbus, with their dedication to Saint Joseph, serve as exemplary models in this regard.

First and foremost, understanding Saint Joseph's role in salvation history sets the foundation for deepening devotion. As the earthly father of Jesus and the spouse of the Virgin Mary, Saint Joseph exhibits a life of silent fidelity and unwavering obedience. Reflecting on his virtues—humility, patience, and dedication—provides profound insights for anyone looking to emulate his path. His silent but powerful presence in the Gospels invites us to listen and act with devotion.

Prayer is the heartbeat of a devotional life. Developing a strong daily prayer routine centered on Saint Joseph can include prayers of consecration, rosaries, or meditations on his life. Incorporating these into the rhythm of one's day ensures constant reminders of his virtues and encourages a state of perpetual mindfulness. This can be as simple as a morning offering to Saint Joseph, invoking his intercession at the start of the day, or meditative reflection on his quiet strength before bed.

But fostering a devotional life goes beyond personal prayer; it's about integrating this spirituality into every aspect of daily living. This means letting Saint Joseph's example guide interactions with family, colleagues, and community members. By emulating his humility and patience, one can transform ordinary moments into acts of grace and kindness. For instance, in challenging work situations, one might pause, invoking Saint Joseph the Worker, seeking his guidance in navigating tasks with integrity and diligence.

The communal aspect of devotion is equally important. Engaging with fellow parishioners or Knights of Columbus members in collective devotion cultivates a shared sense of purpose and spiritual solidarity. Participating in group prayers, retreats, and discussions centered around Saint Joseph can immensely enrich personal devotion. It also fosters a supportive environment where members inspire each other to deepen their faith and live out the values taught by Saint Joseph.

Moreover, instructional resources such as theological writings, hymn books, and visual art dedicated to Saint Joseph can offer more profound insights and inspiration. Reading sacred texts and ecclesiastical teachings about his life provides a richer understanding, thereby deepening one's love and reverence for him. Art depicting scenes from his life, such as the nativity or the flight into Egypt, can serve as visual meditations, prompting contemplation and devotion.

A significant aspect of fostering devotion involves aligning daily actions with the teachings and virtues of Saint Joseph. This can be particularly challenging in a secular world where conflicting values often prevail. However, the unwavering commitment to act in accordance with faith-driven principles can provide a countercultural testament to the power of devotion. Following Saint Joseph's example, one must strive to approach each task, no matter how mundane, with the spirit of dedicated service and quiet excellence.

Regular participation in the sacraments is another cornerstone of a devotional life. Attending Mass, receiving the Eucharist, and participating in the Sacrament of Reconciliation are vital practices that strengthen the soul and fortify one's commitment to a devout life. Through these sacraments, believers remain in close communion with Christ, with Saint Joseph acting as a guiding patriarch, leading them closer to the Holy Family.

Service to others, inspired by Saint Joseph's selflessness, also fosters a robust devotional life. Engaging in acts of mercy and charity, whether through organized community service or spontaneous acts of kindness, illustrates a living devotion. The Knights of Columbus, known for their charitable outreach, provide a model framework, demonstrating how faith in Saint Joseph can inspire meaningful, tangible contributions to society.

Cultivating silence and reflection within one's life is paramount. Inimitable grace is found in quiet moments of contemplation, emulating Saint Joseph's own disposition. Setting aside daily time for stillness allows for spiritual renewal and a deeper connection with God. It's in these moments of peaceful introspection that one can truly hear the gentle whisper of divine guidance, much like Saint Joseph did.

To foster a devotional life dedicated to Saint Joseph, it's essential to balance study, prayer, and action. Each element reinforces the other, creating a holistic approach to living out a consecration. Study without prayer lacks spiritual depth; prayer without action is incomplete; and action without understanding can become misguided. Thus, a true devotional life integrates all three, enabling a more profound journey of faith and dedication.

In summation, fostering a devotional life involves deliberate practices that constantly orient the soul towards Saint Joseph's virtues. Through determination, prayer, community involvement, and living out these values in daily life, one can develop a lasting and meaningful devotion to Saint Joseph. For the Knights of Columbus, this path of devotion isn't merely an aspiration—it's a call to embody the very principles they hold sacred, serving as modern-day bearers of God's divine will, much like their revered patron.

Balancing Secular Duties with Religious Commitments

In a world where the demands of work, family, and social obligations often tug us in different directions, the challenge of balancing secular duties with religious commitments can feel overwhelming. Yet, it is in this very tension that we find the profound example set by Saint Joseph. As the foster father of Jesus and the spouse of the Virgin Mary, Saint Joseph navigated the complex interplay between his earthly responsibilities and his divine vocation with unwavering faith and dedication.

Saint Joseph's life offers a luminous model for modern-day believers, particularly Knights of Columbus, who are called to integrate their faith into every facet of their lives. He did not see his work as a carpenter and his role as protector of the Holy Family as separate or conflicting duties. Rather, he lived in a way that harmonized the secular and the sacred, embodying the principle that one's everyday labor can become a form of worship.

We can draw several practical lessons from Saint Joseph's example. First and foremost, consider the intentionality with which he approached his responsibilities. Whether it was the meticulous craftsman's skill he brought to his carpentry or the vigilant care he showed in protecting Mary and Jesus, Joseph's actions were always imbued with purpose. For the Knight of Columbus, this means engaging in one's work and familial roles not merely as obligations, but as opportunities to serve God.

Moreover, Saint Joseph illustrates the virtue of obedience—not just in grand, visible acts but in the daily, often unnoticed choices. Obedience to God's will does not always require dramatic gestures. Rather, it manifests in the consistency with which we handle daily tasks, treat others with respect, and maintain our ethical principles. Joseph's quiet yet firm adherence to divine guidance serves as a reminder that our religious commitments are to be lived out even in the mundane aspects of life.

The balance struck by Saint Joseph was not a passive equilibrium but an active interweaving of the sacred into the secular. He teaches us that our work is itself a divine calling. This spiritualization of labor is echoed in modern Catholic social teaching, which emphasizes the dignity of work and the importance of integrating one's faith into professional life.

However, achieving this balance requires more than just good intentions. It demands deliberate action and conscious decision-making. Setting aside time for prayer and reflection amidst a busy schedule is crucial. Saint Joseph, though responsible for the temporal welfare of the Holy Family, never allowed his spiritual obligations to lapse. His life exemplifies the need to establish a rhythm of life that accommodates both prayer and action.

For Knights of Columbus, this might mean developing a structured daily or weekly schedule that allocates specific times for prayer, Mass, and other devotional practices. Incorporating religious symbols in the workplace or home can also serve as constant reminders of one's commitment to living a faith-filled life. These small acts, consistently practiced, can greatly aid in keeping religious commitments at the forefront of one's mind.

It's also essential to foster a community that supports one's spiritual and secular life. Saint Joseph was never isolated in his journey; he was a part of the Holy Family, deeply integrated into their communal bond. Knights of Columbus can find strength and encouragement in brotherhood, participating in group activities such as communal prayer, charitable works, and reading Scripture together. Shared experiences in faith can create a supportive network that helps individuals navigate their responsibilities more effectively.

In addition, learning to delegate when necessary is vital. While Saint Joseph shouldered immense responsibilities, he also knew when to depend on divine intervention and the guidance of others. Modern-day Catholics can take a lesson from this by recognizing that asking for help does not signify weakness, but wisdom. Delegating tasks at work or home can provide the necessary space to fulfill religious duties, thereby maintaining a healthier balance.

Another crucial aspect of navigating this balance is understanding the concept of vocation. Saint Joseph's life was a testament to viewing one's daily labor as a vocation—a divine calling rather than just a job. When work is perceived as a path to holiness, it transforms into an offering to God. This perspective can reshape how Knights of Columbus approach their professional and familial roles, viewing each task as a means of growing closer to God.

It's also beneficial to reflect regularly on how one's actions align with the greater mission of serving God's kingdom. Taking time for self-examination and spiritual direction can provide clarity and strengthen the resolve to live out one's faith in all areas of life. This introspection can help to identify areas where secular duties may overshadow religious commitments and allow for course correction.

Furthermore, the balance is also about recognizing the seasons of life and the fluctuation of commitments. Just as Saint Joseph experienced different phases—from the quiet labor in Nazareth to the protective journeys to Egypt—modern Catholics will encounter varying demands. Flexibility, patience, and trust in God's providence are key to navigating these changes gracefully.

The balance between secular duties and religious commitments is not easily achieved; it requires ongoing effort and discernment. Nevertheless, as Knights of Columbus look to Saint Joseph's life, they find hope and practical wisdom. Through intentional living, integration of faith into daily tasks, and the support of a faith-filled community, the elusive balance becomes attainable, allowing the sacred to permeate every aspect of their lives just as it did in the life of Saint Joseph.

Community Engagement through Faith

Community engagement, grounded in the deepest tenets of our faith, serves as a cornerstone for living a life consecrated to Saint Joseph. This engagement doesn't merely consist of sporadic actions but integrates seamlessly into the very fabric of our Catholic identity. Actions driven by faith breathe life into Scriptural mandates and create tangible expressions of God's love for humanity. Saint Joseph's example provides us with a template on how to merge our spiritual aspirations with practical actions within our community.

In examining Saint Joseph's life, we observe a man who was fully engaged with his family and community, yet ever-present in his devotion to God. His quiet and humble servitude provides a robust model for Knights of Columbus who seek to mirror his spiritual and communal dedication. Saint Joseph was not just a guardian of the Holy Family but also a worker whose labor impacted those around him. Similarly, faithful engagement in our communities today should reflect a similar balance of spiritual nurturing and active contribution.

The path to effective community engagement begins with understanding the intrinsic worth of each person as made in the image of God. Saint Joseph demonstrated this through his interactions, always valuing others and dedicating himself to their well-being. Emulating Saint Joseph in this regard, Knights of Columbus can foster relationships rooted in mutual respect and God-centered love. Our faith calls us to extend beyond the church walls, touching lives in meaningful and transformative ways. This necessitates both a hearty spiritual life and readiness to address the practical needs of the community.

One cannot overstate the significance of sacramental life in community engagement. The Eucharist, for instance, is not just a personal devotion but a public testimony of Christ's unifying love. In participating in and facilitating sacraments, we publicly reaffirm our commitment to Christ and each other. Knights of Columbus are encouraged to be active in parish life, promoting and partaking in sacraments, thereby becoming living witnesses of faith to the community. As Saint Joseph nurtured and safeguarded the infant Jesus, so too can we nurture the spiritual growth of our communities through active sacramental participation.

Moreover, fostering a devotional life serves another crucial layer to community engagement. Regular devotions, be they personal or communal, breathe vigor into our collective spiritual life. Whether it's the Rosary, novenas, or specific prayers dedicated to Saint Joseph, these practices unite us in purpose and spirit. They serve as reminders that our actions in the community should flow from a wellspring of divine grace and not merely human effort. When Knights of Columbus lead in these devotions, they reinforce the unity and spiritual health of their communities, mirroring the fortitude and faith of Saint Joseph.

Beyond the spiritual, Saint Joseph also exemplifies the sanctity of labor and the dignity derived from work. In modern society, community engagement through labor can take many forms, from volunteerism to professional excellence with ethical considerations. Working within our communities with a spirit of dedication and integrity becomes a form of worship, an offering to God. Knights of Columbus, in their various vocational roles, have opportunities to serve as shining examples of ethical conduct and faithfulness to divine principles. This work, done in the spirit of Saint Joseph, inspires and elevates the community's moral and spiritual climate.

Engaging the youth and future generations is another pivotal aspect. Saint Joseph, as a fatherly figure, provides a profound example of teaching and nurturing those under our care. Mentorship programs, youth groups, and religious education classes are just some ways Knights of Columbus can foster growth and guide younger members of the Church. By instilling values and leading by example, we not only honor Saint Joseph but also ensure the perpetuation of faith-filled and morally sound communities. It's a direct continuation of Saint Joseph's legacy, safeguarding the Church's future through diligent and compassionate engagement.

A crucial dimension of community engagement also comes through supporting those who experience hardships. The Gospel repeatedly illustrates Jesus' love for the marginalized, and Saint Joseph demonstrated practical compassion and care. We are called to extend this care through acts of charity and justice. This might manifest in food drives, shelter support, advocacy for social justice, or even personal acts of helping a neighbor in need. These actions not only alleviate immediate suffering but also renew hope and faith in the hearts of the afflicted.

Integrating religion into daily life means our faith should guide every decision and action, weaving a tapestry where the secular and sacred coexist seamlessly. Saint Joseph lived a life where work, family, and faith were not separate compartments but interwoven realities. Knights of Columbus are similarly encouraged to live an integrated life. This comprehensive approach doesn't just enrich our personal spirituality but transforms our communities into beacons of God's presence. Such integration ensures our faith remains a dynamic and influential force within our daily lives.

On a broader scale, building and sustaining community initiatives like family support programs or small group ministries furthers the mission of communal engagement. These programs offer consistent opportunities for people to connect, support one another, and grow in faith collectively. Drawing from Saint Joseph's example, Knights of Columbus can spearhead these initiatives, ensuring they address spiritual, emotional, and practical needs, thus fostering a holistic approach to community well-being.

Indeed, the life of Saint Joseph is a testament to the profound impact one individual's faith and actions can have on their community. As stewards of his legacy, Knights of Columbus have a unique calling to embody these principles. Whether through prayer, work, or direct service, every act becomes a testimony of God's love and a means of spiritual enrichment for the community. In this way, community engagement isn't an optional extra; it's an essential expression of our consecration to Saint Joseph.

Ultimately, the synergy between faith and community action defined by Saint Joseph's life provides an aspirational and actionable framework for Knights of Columbus today. As we strive to emulate his virtues, let our commitment to community engagement through faith remain unwavering, robust, and deeply transformative. This balanced approach ensures we honor Saint Joseph not only in our hearts but tangibly in the lives we touch and the communities we serve.

Chapter 11: The Knights of Columbus and Saint Joseph

The Knights of Columbus hold a significant place in the life of the Church, and their mission finds profound resonance in the example of Saint Joseph. As the earthly father of Jesus and the patron saint of workers, Saint Joseph embodies many of the virtues the Knights aim to cultivate: faith, protection, and work ethic. Historically, the Knights of Columbus have always admired Saint Joseph's quiet strength, his unwavering devotion, and his role as a provident guardian of the Holy Family. Through consecration to Saint Joseph, the Knights can deepen their commitment to these virtues, drawing from his exemplary model to navigate the complexities of modern life. This consecration is not just a personal transformation but a collective endeavor, knitting together a community that mirrors the Holy Family's unity and fidelity. Inspired by Saint Joseph's life, the Knights of Columbus continue their mission to protect, defend, and serve, imbuing their actions with the paternal care and diligence that Saint Joseph so aptly displayed.

History of the Knights of Columbus

The Knights of Columbus, founded in 1882 by Venerable Michael J. McGivney, emerged as a beacon of Catholic solidarity and fraternal charity in a time when many Catholic immigrants faced significant hardships in the United States. McGivney, a parish priest in New Haven, Connecticut, sought to address the prevalent social concerns, particularly focusing on the financial instability experienced by Catholic families upon the loss of a breadwinner. His vision materialized into a fraternal benefit society that would not only provide insurance to member families but also embody the virtues of charity, unity, and fraternity.

Initially, the organization faced challenges typical of such pioneering endeavors. There was skepticism about the viability of a Catholic fraternal society among a population already wary of secretive organizations. However, McGivney's steadfast faith and leadership played a crucial role in gathering a group of Catholic men dedicated to the founding principles. The idea of caring for the widows and orphans resonated deeply within the core teachings of the Church, and thus, the Knights began their mission with a strong spiritual backing.

The early years of the Knights of Columbus witnessed a rapid expansion. By the turn of the 20th century, councils were established in numerous states, and membership numbers soared. This growth heralded the beginning of a robust infrastructure aimed at supporting a wide array of charitable activities. From the financial aid offered to families to educational scholarships, the order's efforts mirrored the compassionate heart of Saint Joseph, the protector and provider.

Through its history, the Knights of Columbus have been involved in pivotal moments that shaped both the Church and society. For instance, during World War I and II, the Knights provided comfort and support to soldiers abroad through their "Knights of Columbus Army Huts." These efforts not only bolstered morale but also solidified the Knights' commitment to service in the face of adversity. This tradition of service has continued throughout the decades, extending to various philanthropic endeavors, including disaster relief efforts, support for persecuted Christians, and defending the sanctity of life.

The organization's governance and structural dynamics also evolved to meet the growing needs of its members and the global Church. Supreme Conventions became an essential part of the Knights' annual calendar, bringing together representatives from councils worldwide to discuss strategies, elect leaders, and renew commitments. These assemblies ensure that the Knights remain a democratic body with a clear vision for future growth and service, always aligning their goals with the virtues exemplified by Saint Joseph.

Integral to the Knights of Columbus is their strong emphasis on educational initiatives, reflecting Saint Joseph's role as a teacher of divine wisdom. The organization has invested significantly in academic programs, establishing scholarships and supporting Catholic schools and universities. These educational efforts are aimed not only at promoting academic excellence but also at instilling a deep-rooted spiritual and moral foundation in the youth, thereby preparing future generations to lead with faith and integrity.

The Knights of Columbus have continually adapted to the evolving landscape of social and religious needs. In recent years, this adaptation is evident in their embrace of digital platforms for evangelization and community engagement. Online resources, virtual councils, and digital communications are now part of the arsenal they use to propagate the faith and foster a sense of community among scattered members. This modern approach ensures that the mission of the Knights remains relevant and accessible in an increasingly connected world.

As the Knights of Columbus carry out their mission, they draw inspiration from the life and virtues of Saint Joseph. Known for his unwavering faith and resolute dedication to the Holy Family, Saint Joseph serves as the ultimate model for Knights. His humility, obedience, and protective nature are traits that every Knight strives to emulate. By upholding these values, the Knights align their objectives with a higher spiritual calling, rooting their various endeavors in the ethos of Saint Joseph's paternal care.

The legacy of the Knights of Columbus is also marked by their fervent advocacy for religious freedom. Throughout their existence, they have been staunch defenders of this fundamental right, recognizing that the ability to practice one's faith freely is paramount to living a fully devout life. This advocacy has taken many forms, from legal battles in courtrooms to public demonstrations and diplomatic engagements, continuously striving to protect the liberties that allow both the Church and its members to flourish.

The fraternal bond among Knights is another testament to their rootedness in the values exemplified by Saint Joseph. Brotherhood and mutual support extend beyond mere social interaction; it involves collective spiritual growth, standing together in adversity, and celebrating triumphs as a united body. This sense of camaraderie fosters a robust support network that reinforces the Knight's individual and collective resolve to live out their faith in every aspect of life.

Moreover, the international presence of the Knights of Columbus has transformed them into a global force for good. Their charitable activities span continents, addressing needs from local communities to global crises. Whether it's building homes for the homeless in impoverished nations or providing protection and aid to refugees, their endeavors resonate deeply with the universal call to charity and mercy that Saint Joseph exemplified in his silent yet powerful actions.

As we reflect on the profound impact of the Knights of Columbus throughout their history, it's apparent that their journey is one of persistent faith, unwavering service, and the continuous quest for a deeper understanding of their role in God's divine plan. It stands as a living testament to the possibility of integrating religious devotion with practical charity and communal bonds, much like the quiet strength and enduring love Saint Joseph showed towards his family and, through them, to humanity as a whole.

The Knights' Mission through the Lens of Saint Joseph

The Knights of Columbus, a brotherhood rooted in charity, unity, fraternity, and patriotism, find a profound exemplar in Saint Joseph. Through his life and deeds, Saint Joseph embodies the very virtues the Knights strive to live by. He is more than a symbolic figure; he serves as a spiritual guide and model for fulfilling their mission. Saint Joseph's unwavering faith, humility, and obedience manifest how a devoted life can be wholly consecrated to God's will.

In contemplating the mission of the Knights through Saint Joseph's life, one cannot overlook his role as a protector. Just as Saint Joseph safeguarded the Holy Family, the Knights are called to protect and nurture their communities and families. This protective role encompasses not merely physical security, but also spiritual and moral guardianship. By taking Saint Joseph's protective nature to heart, the Knights are inspired to shield their loved ones from spiritual dangers and guide them toward salvation.

Saint Joseph's unwavering dedication to work resonates deeply with the Knights of Columbus. He toiled tirelessly, not for earthly glory, but to support the Holy Family. The dignity of work, as exemplified by Saint Joseph, is a cornerstone for the Knights. Through their own labor, be it in their professions, charitable endeavors, or ministry, they reflect Saint Joseph's work ethic. This mission is not confined to material provision but extends to fostering spiritual growth and communal welfare. By emulating Joseph's devotion, the Knights transform their daily tasks into acts of worship.

Additionally, Saint Joseph's role as a spouse brings-to-light the ideal of marital fidelity and sanctity. His relationship with the Virgin Mary, marked by mutual respect, love, and servitude, becomes a model for Knightly conduct within marriage. The Knights are encouraged to honor their spouses, uphold the sanctity of marriage, and cultivate a family life grounded in faith. Emulating Saint Joseph's role as a 'just man,' they strive to create homes that are havens of peace and devotion.

Moreover, the Knights look to Saint Joseph as an exemplary father, both in a literal and spiritual sense. Joseph's fatherhood was characterized by selflessness, teaching, and guiding Christ with divine wisdom and love. For the Knights, this translates into a commitment to being present and righteous fathers or spiritual fathers within their community. It is a call to nurture, guide, and instill virtues in their children or those they mentor. The fatherly love of Saint Joseph becomes a template for the Knights, as they seek to affect positive change in their families and communities.

Reflecting on Saint Joseph's obedience to God offers another layer of understanding of the Knights' mission. Joseph's prompt and unquestioning adherence to God's directions, even when they led to unforeseen and arduous paths, speaks volumes. For the Knights, obedience is not a mere compliance but a willing and joyful submission to God's will. This dedication to divine instructions not only strengthens their individual faith but binds the brotherhood in a unified quest for holiness.

In examining Saint Joseph's humility, the Knights find a counterbalance to the modern world's focus on self-promotion. Joseph's humility didn't stem from a sense of inferiority but from a deep-seated understanding of his role in God's plan. This virtue encourages the Knights to act not for personal acclaim but for the glorification of God. The mission of the Knights, therefore, becomes one of silent and faithful service, where the impact is measured not by accolades but by the lives transformed through their humble efforts.

The mission viewed through Saint Joseph's lens extends to community engagement. Joseph was a man integrated deeply into his community, fulfilling his societal duties while adhering to his faith. Likewise, the Knights are encouraged to be active participants in their local areas, standing as beacons of Catholic values. This engagement isn't passive but proactive, addressing the needs of the marginalized, providing charitable assistance, and uplifting moral standards.

A philosophical reflection on Saint Joseph's mission reveals his constant alignment with divine will, a concept deeply embedded in the Knights of Columbus' ethos. Joseph's life was a continuous act of consecration, where every thought, word, and deed was in service of God's plan. The Knights are thus invited to view their mission as a continuous journey of aligning their lives with divine purpose, seeking wisdom in prayer, and fortifying their actions with faith.

Such a mission cannot overlook the virtues personified by Saint Joseph, such as patience, fortitude, and charity. These virtues are not only individual pursuits but are integral to the collective identity of the Knights. In times of trial and adversity, patience becomes their strength, and fortitude their shield. Through acts of charity, they express their profound love for humanity, echoing Saint Joseph's silent but powerful benevolence.

In every aspect of their mission, the Knights of Columbus are called to mirror Saint Joseph's quiet but unwavering dedication to God's call. This reflection through the lens of Saint Joseph transforms their commitments into a sacred duty, underscored by deep faith and a profound sense of purpose. Therein lies the essence of their consecration — to live, act, and love as Saint Joseph did, each becoming a beacon of divine light in a world in desperate need of God's grace.

Ultimately, the integration of Saint Joseph's virtues within the Knights' mission creates a roadmap for a life well-lived in service of God and humanity. It necessitates a continuous self-examination and renewal of vows, ensuring that every action reflects their profound connection to Saint Joseph. This alignment crafts a brotherhood not only steeped in tradition but poised to face contemporary challenges with a resolve nurtured by timeless wisdom.

Chapter 12: Testimonies of Consecration

In reflecting on our spiritual journey, the testimonies of consecrated Knights of Columbus emerge as resounding affirmations of devotion to Saint Joseph. Their narratives, woven with threads of faith, commitment, and transformation, echo the profound impact consecration can have on one's life. Each testimony, a unique tapestry, reveals how aligning one's will with Divine Providence and seeking Saint Joseph's intercession has fortified their resolve, sanctified their daily tasks, and deepened their relationship with Christ. These testimonies not only illuminate the practical implications of consecration but also serve as allegories for the transcendental journey toward holiness, offering invaluable lessons and inspirations for both the laity and clergy alike.

Lessons Learned from Devout Followers

In the journey of consecration to Saint Joseph, the wisdom gleaned from devout followers provides invaluable insights. The experiences of those who have dedicated their lives to Saint Joseph illuminate the path for contemporary faithful, revealing profound spiritual and practical lessons that resonate deeply within the context of Catholic devotion.

One of the most significant lessons shared by devout followers is the importance of unwavering trust in God's providence. Saint Joseph, often depicted as a silent figure in Scripture, exemplifies a profound trust in God's plan, even when it remains shrouded in mystery. Followers who have emulated this trust discuss how their faith has been tested in various ways, whether through personal trials, family difficulties, or professional challenges. They often recount how invoking Saint Joseph in moments of doubt and hardship has strengthened their resolve and deepened their faith. This lesson is particularly poignant for Knights of Columbus, who are called to lead with faith and courage, relying on Joseph's example to navigate the uncertainties of life.

Another critical lesson is the embrace of humility. Saint Joseph's life, marked by simplicity and quiet service, inspires followers to lead lives of humility, rejecting the lure of worldly recognition and pride. This is manifest in the testimonies of those who have dedicated themselves to humility through acts of service within their communities. They share stories of how adopting Joseph's humble approach has led to a more profound union with God, illustrating that true greatness lies in service to others. This lesson aligns seamlessly with the Knights of Columbus' commitment to charity and service.

Devout followers also highlight the value of patience and perseverance. Saint Joseph displayed remarkable patience throughout his life, from the journey to Bethlehem to the flight into Egypt. Followers often reflect on the challenges they have faced where patience was essential—whether waiting for answers to prayers or enduring through slow spiritual growth. They speak of how invoking Saint Joseph's intercession has fortified their spirits, enabling them to persevere through long periods of waiting and hardship. The Knights of Columbus can find inspiration in these accounts, recognizing that patience is a virtue that underpins steadfast leadership and enduring commitment to their cause.

Moreover, followers consistently emphasize the need for obedience to God's will. Saint Joseph's life is a testament to obedient action, whether taking Mary as his wife or safeguarding Jesus. Through prayer and reflection, followers have discerned God's will in their lives, often in unexpected ways. They share how submitting to divine guidance, even when it defies personal logic or desire, has led to greater peace and purpose. This lesson in obedience is particularly pertinent for those consecrating themselves to Saint Joseph, as it underscores the necessity of aligning one's actions wholly with God's divine plan.

The virtue of chastity, modeled by Saint Joseph, is another pillar of the testaments given by his followers. In an era where the understanding and practice of chastity are often misunderstood or undervalued, followers recount how Joseph's pure love for Mary has inspired them to live lives characterized by respect and dignity in their relationships. They speak of the challenges and rewards of embracing chastity, often discussing the inner freedom and spiritual clarity it brings. This lesson serves as a powerful counter-cultural witness, reinforcing the Knights of Columbus' commitment to upholding moral integrity.

Beyond these personal virtues, followers of Saint Joseph also express the importance of family devotion. Saint Joseph, as the head of the Holy Family, provides a model for holy fatherhood and familial leadership. Testimonies often recount how prioritizing family prayer, sacramental life, and mutual support has transformed their homes into domestic churches. They share the fruits of maintaining a consistent pattern of family devotion, emphasizing that it fosters unity, love, and a shared faith journey. Knights of Columbus, as protectors of family values, glean from these experiences a renewed sense of mission in their own family lives.

Community engagement, inspired by Saint Joseph's silently impactful actions, also emerges as a recurrent theme. Followers who dedicate themselves to community service find great inspiration in Joseph's unheralded yet crucial role in salvation history. They speak of their involvement in parish activities, charitable works, and social justice initiatives, seeing these efforts as extensions of Joseph's legacy. These accounts encourage Knights of Columbus to be active participants in their communities, motivated by Joseph's ethos of quiet dedication and impactful service.

Furthermore, followers often recount miraculous interventions attributed to Saint Joseph's intercession. These stories vary widely—from financial providence to healing of illnesses, from finding employment to resolving family conflicts. The common thread in all these accounts is the profound belief in Joseph's powerful intercessory role. Such testimonies bolster the faith of the Knights of Columbus, reminding them of the tangible and miraculous dimension of divine assistance available through consecration to Saint Joseph.

Interestingly, many followers discuss the transformation of fear into faith. Saint Joseph, faced with daunting circumstances, consistently chose faith over fear. Testimonies often highlight moments when followers felt overwhelmed by fear or anxiety, only to find solace and strength through devotion to Saint Joseph. They share experiences of how their prayers were answered in ways that dissipated their fears and bolstered their faith. For the Knights of Columbus, this lesson is invaluable, as it calls them to confront challenges with the same fearless faith exhibited by Saint Joseph.

Devout followers also stress the significance of daily devotion and discipline. They recount how regular prayers, novenas, and meditations dedicated to Saint Joseph have become cornerstones of their spiritual lives. The discipline instilled by these practices fosters a deeper, ongoing connection with Saint Joseph, transforming ordinary days into continuous acts of consecration. This daily devotion is a testament to the enduring nature of faith and provides a blueprint for the Knights of Columbus to integrate into their spiritual routines.

In sum, the lessons learned from devout followers of Saint Joseph are a treasure trove of wisdom. Their experiences offer a roadmap of virtues—trust, humility, patience, obedience, chastity, family devotion, community engagement, miraculous faith, fearlessness, and daily discipline—that are not just theoretical ideals but lived realities. These lessons illuminate the path of consecration, encouraging the Knights of Columbus to emulate Saint Joseph in a life of profound faith and devoted service.

Conclusion

After journeying through this manual, it is evident that the consecration to Saint Joseph provides a transformative path for any Knight of Columbus seeking a closer union with the Holy Family, a deepened relationship with God, and a renewing of spiritual fervor. Let's take a moment to reflect on the profound implications and the overarching themes discussed.

Saint Joseph's life, rich in character and virtue, offers a tapestry of examples that weaves seamlessly into the fabric of Catholic tradition. His silent strength, unwavering obedience, and humble labor resonate deeply with the core commitments of the Knights of Columbus. Throughout history, Joseph's exemplary life has provided a framework for how a devout Christian may navigate the complexities of earthly relationships while keeping eyes firmly fixed on the heavenly goal.

In exploring the importance of consecration, we understood that it's not merely a ritualistic act but a wholehearted devotion, aligning oneself closer to God through the intercessory presence of Saint Joseph. His multifaceted roles—as protector, worker, spouse, and father—each contribute uniquely to this consecration, offering relatable models for Knights to emulate in various aspects of life.

The theological reflections on consecration highlighted the interconnectedness of the Holy Trinity in Saint Joseph's life. By consecrating oneself to God the Father, God the Son, and God the Holy Spirit, through the lens of Joseph, a Knight undertakes a holistic spiritual journey, enriched by the virtues and actions inspired by him. This integrated approach not only reinforces individual faith but also fortifies communal bonds among the Knights.

Understanding and living the Divine Will, as Saint Joseph did, presents itself as a lifelong mission. His life was marked by unerring conformity to God's plan, a trait that imbues every act of duty, no matter how mundane, with divine significance. Embracing this mindset transforms daily hardships and joys into opportunities for deeper spiritual growth and alignment with God's intentions.

Engaging in devout practices and integrating religious life with daily routines bridge the sacred and secular, reflecting Saint Joseph's own existence. The duty of religion requires a persistent, faithful engagement with prayer, sacraments, and virtuous living, ensuring that one's faith permeates all aspects of life, thereby sanctifying mundane activities.

Observance of commandments, mirrored in Saint Joseph's adherence to both divine and natural laws, emphasizes the importance of moral rectitude and ethical living. By aligning actions with Commandments, Knights reaffirm their commitment to God's laws, navigating modern challenges with timeless wisdom and virtue.

The virtues exemplified by Saint Joseph—humility, obedience, chastity, and patience—serve as cardinal guides in striving for holiness. Each virtue, deeply rooted in scripture, provides a reflection for self-improvement and a beacon for leading others. Saint Joseph's quiet humility, steadfast obedience, pure chastity, and enduring patience offer Knights practical tools for daily life challenges.

Adhering to principles of natural law, as highlighted by Saint Joseph's life, reiterates the Catholic understanding that divine order is present in the created world. By living out these principles, Knights conform their lives to a higher moral standard, embodying justice, prudence, temperance, and fortitude.

The original consecration prayers and devotions crafted for this manual are meant to deepen one's relationship with Saint Joseph, offering structured spiritual practices for Knights. These prayers are not mere recitations but acts of the heart, meant to continually renew one's commitment to grow in faith and virtue.

On a practical level, fostering a devotional life, balancing secular and religious duties, and engaging with the community through faith are vital steps discussed. Saint Joseph's example affirms that true devotion is reflected in how one lives out faith in the real world, encouraging Knights to be embodiments of Christ's love in all their endeavors.

The history and mission of the Knights of Columbus, viewed through Saint Joseph's character, find deepened meaning and renewed vitality. His unwavering dedication and selfless service offer an ideal template for Knights as they work to uphold their principles of charity, unity, fraternity, and patriotism.

Testimonies of consecration provide real-world affirmations of the enriching impact that devotion to Saint Joseph has had on countless lives. These narratives inspire, encouraging Knights to pursue their path with confidence and dedication, knowing that Saint Joseph walks with them.

In conclusion, the consecration to Saint Joseph is an invitation to immerse oneself more deeply in the divine mystery, embracing a journey marked by faith, devotion, and transformative grace. For every Knight of Columbus, adopting Saint Joseph's virtues and role as a spiritual guide can profoundly influence one's life, offering a steady compass in navigating the earthly pilgrimage towards eternity. May this manual serve as a beacon, guiding you closer to Saint Joseph and through him, to Jesus and Mary, thereby strengthening your resolve and commitment to live a life of holiness. Amen.

Appendix A: Appendix

This appendix serves as a wellspring of additional prayers and devotions, providing spiritual supplements to deepen your consecration journey to Saint Joseph. Each prayer and devotion here aims to fortify the virtues discussed throughout this manual. Embrace these spiritual exercises within your daily routine, and let them guide you closer to living in accordance with Divine Will. Beyond these revered texts, we've included resources for further study, inviting you to delve deeper into the ecclesial traditions and theological insights that underpin our understanding of sanctity and devoted living. Together, these elements will enrich your spiritual practice and scaffold your devotion to Saint Joseph and your commitment as Knights of Columbus.

Additional Prayers and Devotions

In the sacred tradition of the Catholic Church, prayers and devotions serve as bridges connecting the faithful to the divine. The Appendix's section titled "Additional Prayers and Devotions" presents a unique collection that enriches our manual of consecration to Saint Joseph for the Knights of Columbus. These prayers not only deepen our relationship with Saint Joseph but also echo the timeless traditions and spiritual wisdom passed down through generations.

To begin, we embrace the rich tapestry of traditional prayers dedicated to Saint Joseph. Among these is the Litany of Saint Joseph, an invocation that enumerates his virtues, calling on him as a model of piety, humility, and fortitude. Each title and attribute of Saint Joseph in the litany highlights a distinct facet of his character, inviting the faithful to meditate deeply on these divine qualities and strive to imitate them in their daily lives.

Another integral prayer is the Novena to Saint Joseph. This nine-day prayer is particularly powerful when seeking Saint Joseph's intercession for specific intentions, be they personal struggles, family matters, or vocational discernment. Novenas have historically been a cornerstone of Catholic devotion, offering a structured yet intimate journey through which believers can petition for graces with confidence and perseverance.

Saint Joseph's connection to the Holy Family imbues him with a special grace for intercession in matters of family life. The Prayer for the Protection of the Family invokes Saint Joseph as the protector of families, seeking his guidance and safeguarding for the spiritual, emotional, and material welfare of our households. This prayer emphasizes our reliance on Saint Joseph's paternal care, much as Jesus and Mary depended on him.

In addition to these traditional prayers, contemplative practices such as the Chaplet of Saint Joseph offer a rhythmic and meditative approach to devotion. The chaplet includes a series of prayers and meditations on the mysteries of Saint Joseph's life, similar to the structure of the Rosary. Through its repetitive and soothing cadence, the chaplet fosters a deeper sense of closeness with Saint Joseph, allowing his virtues to resonate in the heart of the devotee.

For those seeking a more interactive form of devotion, the Saint Joseph's Seven Sorrows and Seven Joys draws the faithful into a reflective journey through the pivotal moments of Saint Joseph's life. This devotion juxtaposes his sorrows and joys, underscoring the duality of trials and blessings that every Christian experiences. Through this prayer, one can find solace and inspiration, recognizing that even in sorrow, divine joy can be found.

The Prayer for Workers invokes Saint Joseph the Worker as a model and patron for all laborers. This prayer not only sanctifies the daily toil but also dignifies work as a means to glorify God. It reminds us to approach our labor with the same dedication and love that Saint Joseph exhibited, highlighting the spiritual dimension of work and its role in God's divine plan.

To complement these individual prayers, community-based devotions also hold a special place. The Saint Joseph's Altar, typically arranged during the Feast of Saint Joseph, serves as a focal point for communal celebration and prayer. This traditional altar, replete with symbols of Saint Joseph's life and generosity, also often includes offerings of bread and pastries, reinforcing the themes of providence and charity.

The renewal of sacred bonds occurs through the Consecration to the Holy Family, wherein the faithful consecrate themselves and their families to Saint Joseph, the Virgin Mary, and Jesus. This act of consecration extends beyond individual devotion, fostering a collective commitment to live in accordance with the Holy Family's example, thereby strengthening the fabric of the Christian community.

Finally, immersion in the Scriptures where Saint Joseph's presence is most profound allows for a deeper understanding and appreciation of his role. Reflective Scriptural Meditations dedicated to passages such as the Annunciation to Joseph and the Flight into Egypt provide rich material for prayer and contemplation. These meditations encourage the soul to delve into the nuances of Saint Joseph's faith journey while seeking parallels in one's personal spiritual path.

In summary, the "Additional Prayers and Devotions" section is a treasure trove that offers a range of practices to enhance one's consecration to Saint Joseph. Whether through the rhythmic recitation of the Chaplet, the reflective sorrow and joy of the Seven Sorrows and Joys, or the protective invocation for family and work, these devotions invite the faithful to walk closely with Saint Joseph. They beckon the Knights of Columbus to draw strength, wisdom, and inspiration from Saint Joseph, living out their sacred mission with renewed vigor and holiness.

Resources for Further Study

In this section, we aim to provide you with a comprehensive list of resources for deepening your understanding of Saint Joseph and the practice of consecration. These resources are curated to assist Knights of Columbus, biblical scholars, theologians, and Roman Catholics who want to explore further the profound spiritual themes discussed in this manual.

First, let's explore some essential texts that delve into the life and virtues of Saint Joseph. The Bible remains the primary source for anyone looking to understand his role and significance. Key passages include the Gospels of Matthew and Luke, which illuminate his actions, virtues, and protective nature. For a more in-depth study, consider commentaries that provide historical and theological insights on these texts.

Complementing the biblical accounts, the writings of early Church Fathers such as Saint Augustine and Saint Jerome offer invaluable perspectives on Saint Joseph's life and contributions. Their homilies and commentaries help situate his life within the broader context of Christian theology and tradition.

Modern theological works also offer rich insights into Saint Joseph's significance in contemporary faith practice. For instance, "Redemptoris Custos" by Pope John Paul II is a remarkable apostolic exhortation dedicated to Saint Joseph. It provides a comprehensive analysis of his role in the Holy Family and his continuing importance for the Church today. Another compelling work is "Guardian of the Redeemer," which delves into his multifaceted roles as father, spouse, and protector.

Saint Joseph's association with various virtues is well-documented. To gain a deeper understanding of these virtues, spiritual classics such as Thomas à Kempis' "The Imitation of Christ" and Louis de Montfort's "True Devotion to Mary" offer profound meditations on humility, obedience, and chastity. These works, though not exclusively about Saint Joseph, provide valuable context on how his virtues align with broader Christian ideals.

For those interested in exploring the typological and allegorical dimensions of Saint Joseph, consider delving into "Biblical Typology" by Leonhard Goppelt. While this book covers a range of types and figures in the Bible, it provides a helpful framework for understanding how Saint Joseph prefigures Christ and embodies Old Testament themes in a New Testament context.

The Knights of Columbus have their own rich tradition of devotion to Saint Joseph. Manuals and guides produced by the organization often contain prayers, meditations, and historical information relevant to members. These documents serve as practical tools for integrating the principles discussed in this book into daily life. "The Parish Priest: Father Michael McGivney and American Catholicism" by Douglas Brinkley and Julie M. Fenster is another valuable resource, highlighting the connections between the Knights' mission and Saint Joseph's values.

Academic journals and theological periodicals are vital resources for those who wish to engage with scholarly discussions about Saint Joseph and consecration practices. Notable journals like "Theological Studies," "Nova et Vetera," and "Communio" often publish articles that examine various aspects of Saint Joseph's life and influence. The archived issues of these journals can be a treasure trove of information for the dedicated scholar.

Let's not forget the plethora of online resources available today. The Vatican's official website contains a wealth of documents, encyclicals, and letters related to Saint Joseph. Websites dedicated to Marian devotion often include sections on Saint Joseph, recognizing his integral role in the Holy Family.

For those who prefer multimedia learning, various documentaries and lecture series are available. EWTN (The Eternal Word Television Network) frequently airs programs dedicated to the saints, including Saint Joseph. Programs like "Saint Joseph: Our Spiritual Father" offer visual and narrative journeys through his life and significance.

Additionally, several reputable Catholic publishers produce excellent books and study guides on Saint Joseph. Publishers such as Ignatius Press, TAN Books, and Ave Maria Press have a range of offerings that delve into his life, virtues, and the practice of consecration. Look for titles like "Consecration to St. Joseph: The Wonders of Our Spiritual Father" by Fr. Donald Calloway, which has been highly recommended for those seeking a structured approach to deepening their devotion.

Retreat centers and seminaries also provide unique opportunities for in-person study and reflection. Many offer specific retreats focused on Saint Joseph, where participants can engage in guided meditations, lectures, and discussions. Institutions like the Pontifical John Paul II Institute for Studies on Marriage and Family often include this subject in their curriculum, providing another avenue for scholarly engagement.

For children and younger readers, there are various age-appropriate resources to foster early devotion and understanding. Picture books, biographies, and activity books about Saint Joseph can help inculcate his virtues from a young age. Titles like "St. Joseph, Watch Over My Family" by Nicole Lataif offer engaging ways to introduce children to his life and significance.

Finally, social media and online forums can serve as a platform for community-building and shared learning. Platforms like Facebook, YouTube, and various Catholic forums host groups and channels dedicated to Saint Joseph. Joining these communities allows for the exchange of insights, experiences, and resources, creating a more interactive learning environment.

In summary, the journey of consecration to Saint Joseph is enriched by exploring a variety of resources. From ancient texts and modern theological works to multimedia and community engagement, each offers unique insights and opportunities for deeper understanding. By immersing yourself in these resources, you are not only expanding your knowledge but also nurturing your spiritual life, aligning it more closely with the virtues exemplified by Saint Joseph.

www.ingramcontent.com/pod-product-compliance
Lightning Source LLC
Chambersburg PA
CBHW081405130726
47998CB00011B/3073